Henri·Matisse

k Nude   1935
rose
×36½″
e Baltimore Museum of Art, Cone Collection

Henri Matisse

Texts by

Jean Leymarie, Herbert Read, William S. Lieberman

Retrospective 1966

Organized by

The UCLA Art Council and the UCLA Art Galleries

with the participation of

The Art Institute of Chicago

and the Museum of Fine Arts, Boston

ACKNOWLEDGEMENTS

It is a pleasure to convey the thanks of the University of California, Los Angeles, and my own personal gratitude, to the UCLA Art Council for the Henri Matisse Retrospective Exhibition which the Council has made a reality; and indeed for this beautiful and scholarly catalogue. My deep appreciation is extended to the Matisse family: Madame Georges Duthuit, and Pierre and Jean Matisse. Each member has contributed not only private loans, but also a rich fund of special information, to the end that this retrospective might give a full account of the artist's accomplishments.

This exhibition enjoys the official sponsorship of the French Government under the auspices of the Association Française d'Action Artistique, and I wish to thank all those who have helped in an official capacity, in particular Monsieur Philippe Erlanger, Directeur de l'Association Française d'Action Artistique and Monsieur Edouard Morot-Sir, Cultural Councillor, Representative in the United States of French Universities.

Franklin D. Murphy, Chancellor, UCLA

We are grateful to all those who have helped to make this exhibition possible; they have been generous of their special knowledge, time and cherished possessions. If they have given or lent so freely, they were prompted, we believe, by the desire to share with others, and especially with young people, the kind of happiness that can be drawn from this most luminous performance.

Stated simply, many of us have felt the challenge of this exhibition. We wanted it to be resplendent. We wanted Matisse to stand forth in his own light. Only the best of Matisse, we believed, would be sufficient tribute to him, and this we have tried to assemble. Our goal was to have a large audience see something so admirable, achieved in a cumulative way in this last half century.

Among those who helped, we owe a special debt to Mr. John Maxon and Dr. Harold Joachim of The Art Institute of Chicago; and Mr. Perry Rathbone of the Museum of Fine Arts, Boston; to Dr. Alfred H. Barr, Jr., Mr. Monroe Wheeler and Mr. William S. Lieberman of The Museum of Modern Art, New York; to Monsieur Bernard Dorival of the Musée National d'Art Moderne, Paris; to Mademoiselle C. Audibert of the Musée Matisse, Cimiez-Nice; Mr. James Elliot of the Los Angeles County Museum of Art; to Mr. Joseph H. Hirshhorn and to The Honorable Louis de Cabrol, former Consul General of France, Los Angeles. All in various ways have made exceptional contributions. In particular, Mr. Frank Perls has acted as special consultant on this exhibition for the Art Council. He has worked closely with the Matisse family and has been of the greatest help in the preparing of the catalogue.

Finally, we thank the editors of *L'Œil magazine*, Georges and Rosamond Bernier, who have supervised the production of this catalogue.

Frederick S. Wight, Director, UCLA Art Galleries

CONTENTS

4 Acknowledgements

7 Letter from Henri Matisse to Henry Clifford

9 The Paintings of Matisse   *by Jean Leymarie*

19 The Sculpture of Matisse   *by Herbert Read*

25 Notes on Matisse as a Draftsman   *by William S. Lieberman*

30 Reproductions of the paintings

122 Reproductions of the sculptures

142 Reproductions of the drawings

162 Reproductions of the graphics

170 Reproductions of the découpages

173 Bibliography

178 Exhibitions and catalogues

181 Catalogue of the exhibition

182 *Paintings*

193 *Sculptures*

196 *Drawings*

201 *Graphics*

207 *Découpages*

Henri Matisse   December 31, 1869 - November 3, 1954

Excerpts from a letter by Henri Matisse to Mr. Henry Clifford

We wish to thank Mr. Henry Clifford, former Curator of Paintings,
Philadelphia Museum of Art, and the Philadelphia Museum of Art, for permission to publish
these excerpts, drawn from their catalogue Henri Matisse Retrospective Exhibition
Paintings, Drawings and Sculptures, 1948.

Vence, February 14, 1948

Dear Mr. Clifford:

I have always tried to hide my own efforts and wished my works to have the lightness and joyousness of a springtime which never lets anyone suspect the labors it has cost. So I am afraid that the young, seeing in my work only the apparent facility and negligence in the drawing, will use this as an excuse for dispensing with certain efforts which I believe necessary.

The few exhibitions that I have had the opportunity of seeing during these last years make me fear that the young painters are avoiding the slow and painful preparation which is necessary for the education of any contemporary painter who claims to construct by color alone.

This slow and painful work is indispensable. Indeed, if gardens were not dug over at the proper time, they would soon be good for nothing. Do we not first have to clear, and then cultivate, the ground at each season of the year?

When an artist has not known how to prepare his flowering period, by work which bears little resemblance to the final result, he has a short future before him; or when an artist who has "arrived" no longer feels the necessity of getting back to earth from time to time, he begins to go round in circles repeating himself, until by the very repetition, his curiosity is extinguished.

. . .

The future painter must feel what is useful for his development—drawing or even sculpture—everything that will let him become one with Nature, identify himself with her, by entering into the things—which is what I call Nature—that arouse his feelings. I believe study by means of drawing is most essential. If drawing is of the Spirit and color of the Senses, you must draw first, to cultivate the spirit and to be able to lead color into spiritual paths. That is what I want to cry aloud, when I see the work of the young men for whom painting is no longer an adventure, and whose only goal is the impending first one-man show which will first start them on the road to fame.

It is onlyafter years of preparation that the young artist should touch color—not color as description, that is, but as a means of intimate expression. Then he can hope that all the images, even all the symbols, which he uses, will be the reflection of his love for things, a reflection in which he can have confidence if he has been able to carry out his education, with purity, and without lying to himself. Then he will employ color with discernment. He will place it in accordance with a natural design, unformulated and completely concealed, that will spring directly from his feelings; this is what allowed Toulouse-Lautrec, at the end of his life, to exclaim, "At last, I do not know how to draw anymore."

The painter who is just beginning thinks that he paints from his heart. The artist who has completed his development also thinks that he paints from his heart. Only the latter is right, because his training and discipline allow him to accept impulses that he can, at least partially, conceal.

I do not claim to teach; I only want my exhibition not to suggest false interpretations to those who have their own way to make. I should like people to know that they cannot approach color as if coming into a barn door ("entrer au moulin"); that one must go through a severe preparation to be worthy of it. But first of all, it is clear that one must have a gift for color as a singer must have a voice. Without this gift one can get nowhere, and not everyone can declare like Correggio, "Anch'io son pittore." A colorist makes his presence known even in a simple charcoal drawing.

Yours gratefully, Henri Matisse.

61   Anemones   (1924)
Les anémones
28¾×36¼″
Berner Kunstmuseum, Bern

Jean Leymarie # THE PAINTING OF MATISSE

Painter, sculptor, draftsman, engraver, decorator, theorist—Henri Matisse has made his impact on the whole world for over half a century through the radiance of his art and through his prestige as a thinker and a personality. There are now two museums dedicated to him in opposite corners of France—one in the Northern belfry of his native town, Le Cateau-Cambrésis, and the other on the sunny hillside of Cimiez where, above Nice, he lies at rest in the climate of his choice. Both are monuments to the splendor of his genius and perpetuate the memory he most wished to leave behind: that of *a man who was alive*. "When men have killed joy," taught Sophocles beneath his bright, clear sky, "I do not believe they still live". In an era of confusion and anxiety, which so many artists inevitably echo in their work, Matisse adopts a compensatory vision of "balance and purity", restores the Olympian worship of happiness and glorifies light and its total radiance as the universal source of energy and the infinite principle of change.

In 1890 the twenty-year old Matisse, a grain merchant's son and lawyer's clerk in his native town, suddenly discovered his true vocation, until then unsuspected. To keep him amused during a long convalescence, his mother gave him a box of colors. He was carried into "a kind of paradise", a haven of peace where he felt free to be himself, and where he could find his real world and the direction of his destiny. His first two canvases are sincere and conscientious still lifes of books, one

1

identified by a candlestick. He abandoned his legal career, overcame the resistance of his father and obtained permission to go to Paris for a formal apprenticeship. He spent a short time at the Ecole des Beaux-Arts before entering the celebrated and congenial studio of Gustave Moreau where Rouault was already a student. Here they were joined by Camoin, Manguin and Marquet. As opposed to the prevailing academic tradition, Moreau advocated using museums and streets as subjects. Matisse made about twenty scrupulously exact copies in the Louvre, three of which were after Poussin and five after Chardin, both perennially modern "old masters". Chardin, who at that time fascinated all the painters who came after Manet and Cézanne, also attracted the attention of younger writers, among them Proust and André Gide. The fashion for Dutch interiors influenced

4

Matisse, as in *The Breton Serving Girl*, and in this he was following the example of the Nabis, Bonnard and Vuillard.

Proceeding patiently and methodically, the future colorist turned first to the study of values, or in other words, the study of light variations on a reduced scale of intensity. "A sensitive painter with a fine understanding of the use of grays," his Belgian friend Evenepoel wrote about him on April 12, 1896. He also took pleasure in the sensual differentiations of surface texture, and his still lifes, heavily loaded and interspersed with gleams of light, seize space through condensation. *Still Life*

2

with a Top Hat is a vigorous, realistic interior of a studio, a subject to be repeated throughout his life. The large-size *Dinner Table* (Paris, Collection Niarchos), which Matisse sent to the Salon of 1897, is a landmark because of its technical accomplishment, its textural density and its rich luminosity. For two successive summers in Brittany (in 1896 and 1897 at Belle-Ile) his palette grew lighter and brighter. He was welcomed there by the Australian painter John Russell, a friend of Rodin and the Impressionists, who introduced him to painting in the open air and to the effects of atmosphere. This resulted in a large group of seascapes. Russell presented him with two drawings by Van Gogh, his former fellow student in Paris, and sent Matisse to Pissarro. It was Pissarro who turned him toward color and construction, and warned him against the dangers of the day, the

Numbers in margins refer to reproductions. Footnotes refer to the catalogue of Matisse Retrospective 1966

scientists and the symbolists. Pissarro, who had successively guided or supported the four great creators of modern art, Cézanne, Gauguin, Van Gogh and Seurat, remained open-minded and generous enough to follow and quicken the development of Matisse.

Then began an explosion of color lasting until 1901, a foretaste of Fauvism, strongly pointillist in character. After his marriage in January, 1898, Matisse spent a week in London studying Turner's paintings. He then went to Corsica for six months, where he absorbed the brilliance of the Mediterranean, and lingered for another six months near Toulouse. These were times of relaxation and free experiment after the strict discipline of his studies. He followed his instinct and painted many resonant pictures in pure tones: yellows, emeralds, and reds, the colors taken less from the subject then from his own enthusiasm. There were brightly lit interiors, and landscapes reduced to their simplest elements—trees, houses and gardens caught in the full richness and intensity of sensation . At the end of his stay, Matisse produced an important and curious still life, *Interior: Sideboard and Table*, in which the complex spatial organization is hidden in differing degrees beneath a vibrating screen of intuitive pointillism.   8

Matisse returned to Paris in February, 1899. The death of Gustave Moreau severed his connections with official circles. He used to drag the faithful Marquet from his neighboring studio at 19 Quai St. Michel on joint expeditions, by day enthusiastically painting in the gardens of the Luxembourg or at Arcueil, in the evening sketching in the incisive manner of Lautrec in the cafés and music halls of Montmartre. The heightening of color called for an equivalent directness in drawing. In this graphic domain so essential to the understanding of Fauvism, the role of Marquet must not be underestimated. Marquet had a speed and conciseness worthy of Hokusai, as Matisse was well aware.

As a necessity to his work, but at great sacrifice to himself, Matisse bought an original plaster maquette by Rodin, a canvas by Gauguin, and two pastels by Odilon Redon, a delicate colorist with whom he was on friendly terms. More importantly, he acquired one of the finest versions of the *Bathers* by Cézanne.[1] In fact, the lesson provided by Cézanne's sense of structure and the energy of his colors became Matisse's chief inspiration. He learned from it that "tones are a force in a picture," that the relations and progressions between them must be constructed and balanced. Landscapes and still lifes are built on firm colored planes and conceived in syncopated rhythms that animate space. He then turned his attention to the figure, which he attacked simultaneously in drawing, sculpture and painting. He enrolled at a small academy in the rue de Rennes and met Jean Puy, Derain, and a whole new group of artists who were affected by his dynamism. Over a period of two years, with frenzied violence and astonishing authority, he produced a sensational series of male and female nudes, the contours heavily outlined in black and brutally modeled— hacked out almost—in violets, pinks and cobalt blues. The wild eloquence of these nudes predicts   9 13 certain works by Rouault, who had just received a gift from Matisse of one of his most startling paintings.[2] In March, 1901, at the famous Van Gogh Retrospective in the Bernheim-Jeune Gallery, Matisse was introduced to Vlaminck by Derain. Shortly thereafter he went to Chatou where Vlaminck then lived, and another flame of color was kindled.

From the end of 1901 to the end of 1903, Matisse passed through a somber phase in his life and in his art, burdened as he was by a family and serious material difficulties. His wife was forced to keep a dress shop in order to support the household. He worked at sculpture under the influence of Barye and Rodin, and in his painting temporarily darkened his palette in order to emphasize mass and volume. Matisse's aim was to master a comprehensive language by successive experiments in all mediums of expression, each carried to its conclusion. He would assiduously trace with a plumb line the linear foundations of his figures. The severe modeling and intransigent naturalism of *Carmelina* make it resemble something between Courbet and Vallotton. A few touches of red   16 and blue barely enliven the deliberate neutrality of the ochres and browns. In a background made up of geometric rectangles, a mirror reflects the back of the model as well as the profile of the painter, a device that Matisse would often repeat in the future. From his upstairs window the artist painted several views of Notre Dame and of the Quais seen through a hazy light, in direct emulation of   11 14 Marquet who specialized in such subjects.

In June, 1904, Matisse's first one-man show was held at Vollard's gallery. It was the summary of a long period of study on the eve of a decisive breakthrough. The preface to the exhibition by

---

1. Now in the Petit Palais, Paris, a gift of Henri Matisse.
2. "Study of a man", reproduced "Matisse" by Jacques Lassaigne, Skira (1960) page 36.

Roger-Marx praised the artist's "ruthless demands on himself" and discerned beneath the diversity of his interests "a persistent urge to develop his latent gifts as a colorist." These talents were to flower during the Fauve period after a preliminary encounter with pointillism. This same transitional phase had been necessary to Van Gogh and other great colorists who succeeded him, Kandinsky and Delaunay. Pointillism is a methodical way of intensifying pure color in order to organize a flat surface in terms of fixed basic tone. Matisse spent the summer of 1904 at St. Tropez with Signac and Cross, who were both somewhat rigid followers of Seurat, especially in their oils, for their water colors showed greater warmth and spontaneity. Signac and Cross tried to convert Matisse to their theories. He groped, resisted, made unsystematic attempts, and finally following his own impulse, surrendered to the Mediterranean mood that released him from the bleak tension from which he had been suffering. Soon, color burst forth in glittering cascades.

At that date, there were two rallying points where avant-garde artists could fight their battles: the old Salon des Indépendants held in the spring, of which Signac was the moving spirit, and the new Salon d'Automne founded in 1903. Matisse had participated in the Indépendants since 1901 and had been a member of the Salon d'Automne since its inception. In 1904 he sent to the Salon d'Automne some of the vibrant outdoor studies he had brought back from St. Tropez. During that winter he worked in his studio on an uncompromisingly "divisionist" composition, *Luxe, calme et volupté* (Collection Ginette Signac). This picture is a synthesis in which he is concerned simultaneously with contrasts of tone, color and line. The title itself is taken from Baudelaire, the poet-creator of modern sensibility to whose writing Matisse was deeply responsive. Actually it is more descriptive of his later work than of this particular canvas, which depicts bathers picnicking by the sea. This painting-cum-manifesto was purchased by Signac, and became the center of attraction of the Salon des Indépendants of 1905. When Dufy saw it, he was profoundly struck by "the miraculous imagination of the draftmanship and the color." Thus Matisse detached himself from his contemporaries to lead a younger radical generation in the twentieth century revolution.

In the summer of 1905 he went to Collioure on the Roussillon coast, taking with him Derain who was ten years his junior and the habitual companion of Vlaminck at Chatou. For the next decade Matisse was to return faithfully to this little Catalan port, its pure, densely packed shapes cradled behind its ramparts between the sea and the mountains. Its name is often used to denote the period of his highest achievement before his final liberation. Derain's letters to Vlaminck describe the beauty of the place and the importance of being there, as well as the rewarding collaboration between himself and Matisse. He wrote of the transformation their work underwent in the brightness "of a yellow, golden light which eliminates shadows." Matisse and Derain paid frequent visits to the sculptor Maillol, their neighbor at Banyuls. Maillol spoke in glowing terms of the nobility of the region which seems ever present in the Arcadian painting *Pastoral*. He related his personal memories of Gauguin, affirmed his admiration for him, and took Matisse and Derain to see the collector Daniel de Monfreid who lived nearby and owned some sumptuous, unknown works by Gauguin from the South Sea Islands. These canvases, painted in supple curves and broad color planes, were a revelation to Matisse at a decisive moment. He broke away from the strictures of pointillism. However confined he had felt by its limitations, he had still continued to explore its possibilities in his way, but now he began to paint in flat areas of pure color in order to create space and light. The last canvases painted at Collioure, like the *Open Window* (New York, Collection John Hay Whitney), present an inventive combination of sparkling pointillist techniques and single-color areas.

Immediately upon his return to Paris, swept on by his new excitement, Matisse produced one of his most vivid canvases, *Woman with the Hat* (Madame Matisse). The fantastic purple hat adorned with many-colored feathers crowns a mottled pink and green face and vermillion hair. There is no longer any differentiation between the figure, the dress, and the background. All has become part of the same flamboyant whole. Through this very fact, the character and the individuality of the face are accentuated all the more, and we are greeted by the compelling gaze of the then recently discovered figures of Fayum or El Greco. This spectacular picture was the principal attraction and target of the historic Salon d'Automne of 1905, where Matisse and his friends created a scandal and were labeled the "Fauves." The *Woman with the Hat* was followed by a second portrait of Madame Matisse, bareheaded this time, in which the grandeur and unity of the new style are mastered. This picture was entitled *The Green Line (Madame Matisse)* (Copenhagen) because of the audacious central line that divides the light side of the face from the dark, giving both light and relief without recourse to the illusionist techniques of shadows and modeling. The colors, instead of fusing together from scattered sources as before, are massed into clearly defined separate zones and reverberate at their maximum intensity. "Fauvism was for me," Matisse said, "the testing of the tools: I had to place side by side and put together in an expressive and meaningful way a blue, a red and a green." The composite of flecked brush strokes and transparent water-color effects reappeared a little later in *Reading*[3] without detracting from the unity of the whole. The girl, absorbed in her book, is an integral part of all the objects that surround her, all bathed in an equal light.

This canvas appeared in Matisse's second one-man show in March, 1906, at the Druet Gallery where the multiple aspects of his art were brought together—paintings, sculpture, drawings, a series of lithographs, and three woodcuts. This exhibition was eclipsed by the overwhelming presence at the Salon des Indépendants of a major composition entitled *Joy of Life* (Barnes Foundation), at once the symbol and triumphant condensation of Matisse's art and the first supreme monument of our century before its nocturnal counterpart Picasso's *Demoiselles d'Avignon*. It unites in an extraordinary synthesis the two traditionally opposing themes of the pastoral and the bacchanal. At one and the same time it glorifies Dionysian elation and Apollonian peace, rhythm and melody. *Arabesque* and pure tone create their own musical space together, with no concern for naturalism. The painting was immediately acquired by Gertrude and Leo Stein, who already owned *The Woman with the Hat*, while Michael and Sarah Stein had reserved *The Green Line (Madame Matisse)*.

Matisse was often entertained in the cosmopolitan apartments of the rue de Fleurus and the rue Madame, and it was there that he met the young Picasso against whom he would pit himself for fifty years. The story of this confrontation and its strong interactions has not yet been written. There soon appeared other American admirers, among them Harriet Lane Levy[4] of San Francisco, the sisters Claribel[5] and Etta Cone, whose collection was to become a gem of the Baltimore Museum; and the Bostonian archaeologist, Thomas Whittemore,[6] who later discovered the mosaics of Saint Sophia. Whittemore's passion for the art of Matisse opened his understanding of the art of Byzantium and vice versa.

After the two exhibitions at Druet's and the Indépendants, Matisse, already sympathetic to the freshness and stylization of Islamic art, took his first trip to North Africa, a region that had attracted painters in search of color since Delacroix and Renoir. He paid a brief but stimulating visit to Biskra, a place that also inspired Gide, whose paths and ideas were to some degree parallel to his own. Matisse brought back from Biskra Arab ceramics and textiles which often figured resplendently in his future pictures. He then returned directly to Collioure, where he stayed until the end of the summer. With unflagging energy he spread his activities in every direction, working over a great range of techniques: splashes, flat colors, dots, and translucent or saturated areas. His forms were sometimes massive and heavily outlined, sometimes fluid and free. Again, he would leave narrow white strips of bare canvas between them in order to allow his colors to breathe, as in the magnificent *Still Life with Geranium Plant and Fruit*. For the first time he adopted a procedure he would often repeat: he painted in succession two like-size, but different versions of a *Young Sailor*, one angular and somber, the other serene and bright, its curvilinear rhythms expanding with oriental ease.

At the Salon d'Automne of 1906 (which coincided with the largest retrospective of Gauguin ever organized) all the Fauves were grouped around Matisse in their fullest and most brilliant array. In the words of the critic Vauxcelles, it was "a real fireworks display." But the violence of the color was less important than the change in purpose. "That is only the superficial aspect," declared Matisse. "Fauvism sprang from the fact that we got far away from colors of imitation. By using pure colors only, we achieved more powerful results—simultaneous results which were more immediate; and there was also the *luminosity* of the colors." It was a question of going further than Gauguin in an even more systematic way without any literary compromise or nostalgia for volume. Matisse was handling areas of pure flat colors complete in themselves. These were linked as much to imagination as to reality, and were capable of creating space and of rendering the energy and *significance* of objects. Fauvism was in tune with the contemporary philosophy of intuition, of Bergson's vitalism. "I am unable to distinguish between the feeling I have for life and my way of expressing it," confessed Matisse. Form and content were wholly united in the body of an unbroken surface which had no hierarchy or divisions, for "expressiveness springs from the colored surface which the spectator grasps in its entirety."

The dawning century was reaching toward a global view of nature, as well as toward the complete

22

23

24

3. See drawing No. 141.   4. See drawing No. 159.   5. See drawing No. 176.   6. See drawing No. 186.

revitalization of history. Matisse, by instinct and by education, was at the heart of this dual movement. He drew more and more upon the arts of oriental countries and primitive societies, insofar as they symbolized the profound relationship between man and the universe. The arts and responses that had been destroyed by western rationalism, ceased to be "exotic" in his eyes, and became "historic" and fully integrated into the universal tradition. It was no longer necessary to go into romantic exile in order to relive lost myths. One only had to travel widely.

The year 1907 marked a turning point, the beginning of Expressionism and the birth of Cubism. Out of these contradictory tendencies appeared the formidable *Blue Nude* (Baltimore) which Matisse completed for the Salon des Indépendants. He then visited Italy, pausing longest before Duccio, Giotto and Piero della Francesca, all masters of color and monumentality. Among other paintings he sent to the Salon d'Automne (where the Cézanne Retrospective had succeeded Gauguin's), were the first version of *Luxe* (Paris, Musée National d'Art Moderne), and the small, richly suggestive sketch for *Music*. In these, he attempted to resolve the relationship between the figures and their bright background by unifying and reducing them to their essentials. In an article devoted to him that December, Apollinaire praised "the strength of his simplicity and the softness of his light." These qualities are visible in a definitive composition of 1908, *Bathers with a Turtle*. [7] Here the background is simplified into three horizontal strips: the sand, the sea and the sky. The little red-brown creature is the vivid focal point centering the attention of three figures spaced out over the canvas. In turn it holds the attention of the spectator. That year at the Salon d'Automne a separate room was devoted to Matisse, and his works were also exhibited in London, Berlin, Stockholm, New York and Moscow.

Matisse was persuaded to open an art school for foreign students which flourished until 1911. On December 25, 1908, he published in the *Grande Revue* his much-quoted *Notes d'un Peintre*, which created a considerable stir. As with Delacroix or Poussin, a critical awareness equal to his creative invention testifies to his accomplishment. He gives us, at a period of highest fulfillment, the definition of his aesthetic. "I want to reach that state of condensation of sensations which constitutes a picture," he declared, and in this he succeeded during the next decade.

From 1909 to 1917 he withdrew to the outskirts of Paris to a large, quiet house in the middle of a garden at Issy-les-Moulineaux, on the road to Clamart. Over these years (in a setting described by Clara T. MacChesney in the New York Times of March 9, 1913) he executed major works whose majestic serenity was the outgrowth of bitter struggles. Although he pursued his solitary conquest of the sun, in the face of the adverse rise of Cubism, his association with contemporary trends was much closer than is generally understood. For example, in August aud September, 1913, he went horseback riding in the woods of Clamart with Picasso at a time when they seemed in greatest opposition; the following summer he was joined at Collioure by Juan Gris. The Synthetic Cubists were beginning to use color, even to the point of decoration, at the very moment when Matisse partially abandoned it in order to concentrate on architectural structure. They all benefited mutually from an exchange of ideas. In 1912 the Bernheim-Jeune Gallery, which represented Matisse, hailed the Italian futurists; one of whom, Severini, remained in Paris and became a friend of Matisse. Matisse's journeys to Germany and Russia put him in contact with the artists of these countries. During these crucial years, Matisse was largely responsible for the success of experiments in color and form which also preoccupied Kandinsky, Delaunay, Chagall, Villon and Léger.

Having restored the magnetic dynamism of color, the painter broke down its substance and turned to the dazzling examples of the Orient, where all forms of art, from mosaics to textiles, from icons to ceramics, are traps to catch the light; he converted color into light; he dedicated himself to light. If Impressionism is atmosphere, and Fauvism color, Matisse is the creator and worshiper of light. His visit to the large exhibition of Islamic art in Munich in October, 1910, his trip to Moscow in 1911, where he discovered and admired the icons, his prolonged stays in Andalusia and Morocco during the winters of 1910 to 1913 in the heart of a culture where the sun is law, stimulated him and confirmed his direction. "Inspiration has always come to me from the Orient," he stated. "Persian miniatures... revealed to me all the possibilities of my senses. Because of its dense detail, this art suggests a larger space, a truly plastic space, and it helped me to go beyond intimate painting."

In reaction against the tradition of easel painting and its small-scale subtleties, Matisse felt the need to experiment with the spaciousness of murals. He received some private commissions which

7. See drawing No. 149.

gave him the desired opportunity. At the request of his Russian patron Sergei I. Shchukin,[8] the most important collector of the pre-World War I period, he executed the two panels *Dance* and *Music*, which created a sensation at the Salon d'Automne of 1910 before being installed in Moscow. Conceived in highly expressive *arabesques*, in only three colors, blue for the sky, pink for the figures, and green for the hill, they personify the universal principles of Dionysian motion and ecstatic contemplation. In the one, the dancers straddle the globe in a single, continuous leap and in the other the musicians and their listeners are immobilized in space like notes on a stave. The remarkable full-size study of *Dance*,[9] painted as early as 1909, is primarily a study of color applied to the saturation point and brought to the highest intensity. After the *fin de siècle* mists and melancholy, the reinvigorating vitality of such a work serves as the most effective answer to the growing forces of destruction and death.

29

In 1911, Matisse painted a composition in tempera for Michael Stein, *Interior with Eggplants*, which the artist subsequently presented to the Museum of Grenoble. Here, in contrast to *Dance*, there is a proliferation of ornament over the entire surface of the canvas. Three eggplants on the table add a note of weight to the rich composition. The writer, while curator of the Museum of Grenoble, looked at this masterpiece for a long time. Its affinities with Chinese painting have already been pointed out. Curiosity about its mystery resulted in the discovery that oriental wisdom holds the belief that a dream of three eggplants is a symbol of happiness. One remembers Matisse's joy when told of this proverb; it so aptly complemented his inspiration and his intuitive discovery which he had made simply by following the laws of color. "Imitate the Chinese with a serene and sensitive heart...," he liked to quote this line by Mallarmé, his favorite writer apart from Baudelaire, whose *Poésies* he was also to illustrate. In 1911 the dress designer Poiret, baffled, refused to accept a decorative painting intended for him, *The Blue Window*. It is the view from the painter's bedroom at Clamart transposed into a Persian and Moroccan fantasy, a nonrealistic modulation of blue with accents of green, punctuated by the red of a carnation. A window is one of the characteristic motifs of the painting of that time (i.e., Bonnard, Delaunay, Gris) as well as of the poetry (i.e., Mallarmé, Apollinaire, Rilke). Throughout his work, in different ways at different periods, Matisse made highly ingenious use of it. Instead of deepening the perspective in the traditional manner, Matisse's windows bring the composition forward to its frontal plane, in other words, to the plane of the canvas itself, of which the window is also the image by its very form. It loses its function of *trompe l'œil*, or means of escape, to become a visual compressor and sensitive amplifier, a pliable link between the inside and the outside, the enclosed and the infinite.

31

The masterly group of interiors completed in 1911 includes a composition of figures set against an elaborately patterned background; *The Painter's Family* (Leningrad) and two interiors show studios without figures but filled with works of art—mainly sculptures which appear more alive then beings of flesh and blood. The Leningrad version is crammed with gaudy materials and carpets, but the *Red Studio* of New York is boldly controlled by a flat red monochrome which covers the whole canvas. It is impossible to carry further the reduction of volume to the level of the picture surface, all the while magically suggesting the depth of a whole room. After this decorative exuberance, Matisse returns to simplicity until 1919. The theme of the studio, which permits the artist to dramatize the mystery of creation, obsessed Matisse unendingly, as it did numbers of other contemporaty painters. Like the motif of the window which he frequently used, the studio presents another opportunity for justifying the ambiguity of a painting within a painting: the dialogue between art and reality. From January, 1914, onward, Matisse took another winter studio in his old building in Paris. It can be recognized from the window facing the quays appearing in two powerful works of 1916, *Studio, Quai St. Michel* and *The Painter and his Model*, characterized by severe structure and subdued colors.

41 49

The same Italian model, Lorette, posed for both, lying nude on a red sofa in one, and dressed in green sitting in a mauve armchair in the other, just as she appears in her portrait of the same date on a dark background. In the version where the painter has his back turned, there is extreme tension between the interior and the exterior, between the painter and model, and her likeness on the easel. The baroque curves of a superb Venetian mirror on the empty wall counterbalance the geometric austerity of the composition.

44

Paralleling these studio scenes, comes the dazzling and varied series inspired by Tangier: gardens, views of cities, still lifes, and native figures of ferocious dignity or graceful reserve. The series culminates in a monumental synthesis, *The Moroccans* (New York, The Museum of Modern Art).

32 34

8. See drawing No. 157.   9. See drawing No. 151, 152.

The various elements that Matisse has drawn from memory—architecture, nature, turbaned figures —are reduced to their bare essentials and produce a complete harmony which suggests at once the luxuriance and spirituality of the Moslem world. The sensation of intense light and moral certitude is rendered by a dominant black, the summation of all color, which stands for inner strength. The same process of clarification and crystallization operates in *Piano Lesson* (New York, The Museum of Modern Art), where the basic color is a subtle gray which emphasizes the geometry of the colored planes. Master of the *arabesque* and of pure color, Matisse is also the equal of the Cubists in his brilliant invention of compositional rhythms and plastic symbols. He has been criticized, and precisely in connection with these supreme successes, for going too far toward abstraction, or for not having dared to go far enough. But the dispute is meaningless. His greatest creations reveal, in his own words, a "spiritual space" which overcomes all constraint and duality and reconciles the internal and external, moving away from ourselves toward the world, rather than from the world to ourselves. His mastery is equally evident in his vast, vigorously studied compositions and in the few simple and poetically fresh landscapes, for example, *Tree Near Trivaux Pond*. It also shows in the quieter still lifes such as *Lilac Branch*, and the paintings, *The Pewter Jug*, which are wonders of shimmering grace and concentrated strength. This aspect of Matisse's work is too little known.

"What interests me most," Matisse stated in 1908, as if echoing Van Gogh, "is neither still life nor landscape, but the human figure. It is through it that I best succeed in expressing the almost religious feeling I have towards life." Throughout his career he had been drawing portraits, but the portraits in oil were nearly all painted in the period we have just covered, bracketed between the two sober and resolute self-portraits of 1900 and 1918. They reflect the range of his style, but at the same time they draw from each human face its individual quality and its "character of high seriousness." Most numerous and outstanding are the portraits of his wife, reaching a climax of Fauve intensity in 1905 and classical unity in 1913 (Leningrad); and those of his daughter, *Marguerite*,[10] which are sometimes formal and stylized like effigies at Ravenna or Baouit or else hallucinatory in their direct, realistic approach. A portrait demands "the complete identification of the painter with his model," declared Matisse. "It is by getting inside the subject that one gets inside one's own skin." The portraits that convey the strongest likenesses are always those in which he himself looks at us through the eyes of his model. The small study of *Pierre Matisse* as a child in a fisherman's jersey, painted during the summer of 1909 at the same time as the study for *Dance*, is marvelously exact and succinct. In the *Girl with Green Eyes*, painted in the fall of the same year and immediately acquired by Miss Harriet Lane Levy of San Francisco, the subject stands facing forward, bright eyes in a pale face, against the rich texture of the related background. By contrast, the full length portrait of *Yvonne Landsberg*,[11] widened spatially by strange radiating curves, and that of the actress *Greta Prozor*,[12] are impressive because of their linear density and subdued colors: steel gray and dark blue. *White Plumes*, the masterpiece of the Museum of Gothenberg (another version at Minneapolis),[13] is the 1919 decorative equivalent of the *Woman with the Hat* of 1905. Under her superb baroque hat assembled by the painter himself, the attractive face of the model, Antoinette, ceases to be just a portrait and is assimilated into the rhythmic perfection of the composition. From then on Matisse reigned over an ideal world from which the agitation and burden of individual characterization are removed.

Nothing illustrates the change of style and climate better than the comparison between *The Painter and his Model* in the 1917 Paris version, already mentioned, and another version of the same subject done in Nice after an interval of two or three years. The tension and force in the former give way to grace and ease; the monastic austerity of a winter studio is replaced by a flower-filled room where the light is filtered and an odalisque occupies the place of honor. The painter is effortlessly included in the picture which he relishes and directs. "I very often put myself in my paintings and I am aware of what is behind me. I express the space and the objects that are arranged in it as naturally as if I were facing only the sea and the sky; that is to say, in the simplest possible way."

From 1917 onward Matisse spent long periods in Nice. He settled there permanently in 1921, in the clear and serene light that irradiated the second half of his life. Shortly before Renoir died Matisse showed him his canvases. Renoir was particularly struck by the trueness of his colors and the miraculous way in which they fixed each plane at the desired distance.

45
38 46 47

10 50

15 18
22 30 40 48

28

27

35
39
51

49
52

10. See drawing No. 155.
11. See etching No. 242.

12. See drawing No. 161; drypoint No. 260.
13. See drawings No. 163-165.

Matisse now enjoyed a period of relaxation which followed the end of the war and lasted until 1925. Like Braque and Picasso, he reverted to a more naturalistic conception, delighting in his own virtuosity. If there is a profusion of odalisques,[14] they combine to make a coherent series which should be looked at as a whole. The orientalism in Matisse is not exotic or mannered, but is a necessity of his nature and an outcome of a style based on his experiences in Morocco. It crystallizes his Baudelarian dream of the odalisque-woman, "a divinity, a goddess who presides over the consciousness of the masculine brain." Her body is an *arabesque*, her clothing a symphony of color, and the setting she requires becomes a receptacle for light. Moreover, this period is as strong as others in important compositions. *The Interior at Nice* from Chicago, with the figure on the balcony significantly turned inward and not out toward the sea; the *Moorish Screen* with its softness of color, *Checker Game and Piano Music*, the organization as supple as it is infinitely complex, demonstrate the powerful ability of Matisse to renew his treatment of space and ornamentation, and to re-explore the relationships between figures and objects.

With the increased depth, and interplay between the interior and the exterior, light becomes the predominant element. The window subtly regulates the amount of light by its transparent or opaque curtains, and by the Mediterranean shutters whose role has been so cleverly described by a friend of Matisse, the poet André Rouveyre: "They appear in his canvases as movable boundary lines between his unlimited horizon and his private world. The shafts of sunlight break or dissolve against them, are blunted, pierce through slightly, or penetrate deeply. They represent the point where his field of spiritual and visual sensibility begins, where his thoughtful emotions and arpeggios of color originate, and where very frequently women appear, clothed or naked, but always subordinated to something latent yet imperious, which is the sovereign authority of a prince in the exercise of his art."

After 1923 Matisse turned to the discipline of sculpture, and began to recover the solidity of his inventive structures and the intensity of his colored planes. This becomes visible in *Nude Seated on a Blue Cushion*,[15] and in *Odalisque with Tambourine* (Collection William S. Paley), a rhythmic mass illuminated by fiery reds. It reached its climax in 1927-28 in a vigorous series of still lifes, nudes and odalisques,[16] among them an outstanding canvas bearing the revealing title *Decorative Figure on an Ornamental Background*[17]. The commonplace model is transformed into an idol, her pyramidal form rising in the midst of an extravagantly profuse décor which provides balance without overwhelming her. It is the extreme case of the problem Matisse confronted so often—the struggle and harmony between figure and background. For this painting, the figure is justly described as "decorative" because it has ceased to be a privileged subject and has simply become a unifying element. "Composition," said Matisse, "is the art of arranging in a decorative way the various elements which the painter has at his disposal to express his feelings." *Girl in a Yellow Dress*, begun in 1929 and finished in 1931, is an exceptional transitional work, with its central and frontal pose of the model, almond-shaped in the window bay with shutters half-closed, and with its basically ochre and lemon-yellow color orchestration. Between 1930 and 1933, Matisse's time was taken up with traveling to and from America, and with his three months' visit to Tahiti, when he "stored up impressions" in the "golden light" of the Pacific. He was concentrating on illustrations for Mallarmé (he dedicated a panel to Mallarmé, *Nymph in the Forest*, never shown until the Henri Matisse Retrospective of 1966) and on the huge undertaking of the murals for Barnes on the persistent theme of the *Dance* which he entirely reworked and transformed. The *Portrait of a Lady in White* is one of the rare and better paintings of the years 1933-1934, before the unfolding of *Still Life with Three Vases* in 1935 and some monumental nudes, posed by a splendid new model, Lydia. *The Dream* is a triangle of the model's sleeping head resting on her arms, the arms forming the base. A canvas of prime importance is the *Pink Nude*. The model lies on a blue couch in a composition that went through twenty successive states before its final resolution. It displays the majesty of organic form fused with its setting, rounded volumes fused with flat planes, proud tension with complete repose.

The year 1937 saw the creation of some brilliant decorative paintings characterized by broad surfaces saturated with pure uniform colors and covered with fine networks of lines. Two aristocratic, complementary beauties posed for them, the blond Lydia and the dark Helena, Princess Galitzine.

14. See drawing No. 167; litho. No. 269-273, 277, 279, 281, 283.
15. See drawings No. 166, 168; lithos. No. 277, 281, 285, 286, 276.
16. See drawing No. 169, 171; litho. No. 291.
17. See drawing No. 172.

76 78
They are dressed to suit their coloring and their oriental charm, in Rumanian blouses and Persian jackets or long, full, so-called period dresses adorned with amber or sparkling jewels. After immortalizing woman "in the way she looks and the way she moves her limbs", Matisse (again quoting Baudelaire) honors "the endless shimmering clouds of material in which she swathes herself, at once the attributes and the pedestal of her divinity". In these paintings, elegance never falls into conventionality because it shines over the entire picture, elongations and distortions included; the shape of the hair is repeated in a bunch of leaves or a hand threaded with black pearls riding on the blue billow of a dress. In 1938 and 1939 Matisse was mainly occupied by commissions for designs (the Rockefeller fireplace decoration, the designs for the Monte Carlo Ballet) and continued this same

79
style in some two-figure compositions, the most notable being *Music* in Buffalo. Two canvases of 1940 reveal his supreme mastery of both still life and figure painting, of fluid, transparent color and

80
expressive *arabesques*. One of these, *Pineapple and Anemones*, was painted in February; the other,

81
Sleeping Woman [18], in September after the defeat and the invasion, a fact which doubtless contributes to its moving character.

In March, 1941, when he was over seventy, Matisse underwent a serious operation, the outcome of which was uncertain. In spite of pain and confinement to bed, he lived out the fourteen years remaining to him as an unexpected extension of time, and determined to make them a hymn of joy. On the hilltops of Vence or Cimiez, among his plants and rare birds, surrounded by his precious vases and Oriental textiles, he became, in the fullness of his genius, "the calm and beautiful old man surrounded by unparalleled abundance" of Rimbaud's dreams. The flowering began in 1941 with

82
some dazzling still lifes and continued in 1942 with the figure paintings in which black becomes the richest color against the lemons and lacquers, and the rococo armchair becomes the partner to the

83
slender dancer.

At the beginning of 1943 some fine variations appear on the theme of a young woman dressed in white, sitting in a red and blue interior to the left of a table decorated with fruit and flowers. In one

85
of the two most complex and elaborate versions, the girl carefully plays her *Lute*. In the second, she sits pensively on a chair, which acts as a balance to the same lute placed on another chair, and to

86
the table with still lifes that include a jar inscribed *Tabac Royal*. The mauves and the whites hold their own against the excitement of the reds and blues by means of the lemon yellows.

For several years Matisse concentrated on book illustrations. *The Interieur in Yellow and Blue*

87 88
91
89
(1946) is the first of his final series of interiors which blossoms in 1947 into small-size poetic variations and concludes in the spring of 1948 with six vast, definitive compositions. Two of the most significant are *The Pineapple*, a sensual concentration on a single object caught in its surroundings, and *Large Interior in Red*, essentially a diffused light in a rhythmically ordered "spiritual space". Both recall and summarize the dual approach of the artist. *The Pineapple* reappears as a picture-

90
217
inside-the-picture on the wall of *Large Interior in Red*. Here it is paired with a drawing in Chinese ink of a landscape that looks like a window. The black and white of the drawing sets off the brightness of the color. This painting is the synthesis and climax of his entire work.

92
If we except his last canvas, Matisse deliberately gave up oil and easel painting in 1951. In his eighties he invented simpler, more radiant techniques. From 1948 to 1951, he concentrated his energies on the Chapel [19] at Vence as an act of thanks and as a legacy to mankind. It was a monumental project undertaken in its entirety, encompassing architecture and decoration, including the stained-glass windows, ceramics, and liturgical vestments. He said his chief aim "was to balance a colored, illuminated surface with a solid white wall covered with black drawings." From 1950 until the death of Matisse in November, 1954, these magnificent pen or brush drawings in Chinese ink alternate

346
with pure gouache on paper, cut out directly with scissors. These cut-and-pasted paper creations (*gouaches découpées*) represent his most daring contribution to the art of his time. Unlike the Cubist or Surrealist collages, his paper cutouts consist of solid, fixed elements: form, color, light, bound indissolubly and wedded to the mural support of the actual wall, through the rightness of their interrelationships and outlines. There is no longer any perspective or other depth except the indestructible link between the artist and his creation. Matisse more than justifies the prophecy of his teacher, Gustave Moreau, "You will simplify painting". He anticipates the most vital present-day experiments in speed and improvisation which are based on direct contact with the medium and on the demands of decoration. In order to achieve such freedom, "one must, of course" he noted, "have one's entire experience behind one and not have lost the freshness of instinct".

18. See drawing No. 190.   19. See drawings No. 218, 219.

The whole work of Matisse is epitomized in his final simplicity and radiance. He rejoiced in the translucent blue of sea and sky, the flowers and fruits of the earth, the inexhaustible *arabesque* of a woman's body, and the circle of the sun. On the eve of his death he brought to life his dazzling visions of Tahiti. Mastery of these paper cutouts enabled him to hint at the vast and limpid Polynesian space and the irridescence of lagoons in what he called a painter's paradise. The light of the Pacific transfigures his final accomplishment and justifies his profoundest wish: "I have attempted to create a crystalline environment for the spirit."

Other artists since Rembrandt, such as Matisse's friend Rouault, have interpreted light and shade as the condition of the Christian soul whose light is by turns withheld and released. Henri Matisse is the pagan poet of light-without-shade, shining and serene. "Il porte un soleil dans le ventre", said Picasso: a sun whose thousand rays light up a rainbow of happiness in our storm-ridden sky.

Translated by Caroline Lumley

Herbert Read # THE SCULPTURE OF MATISSE

Painting and sculpture are both "plastic" arts, and are called such because the concern of the artist is to render the three-dimensionality of objects. This elusive quality is perhaps more easily obtained in works of sculpture which inevitably occupy space, but even sculpture can be flat and inert. The painter achieves an effect of plasticity by tonal contrasts, especially those created by the representation of light and shade. With the advent of Impressionism the painter renounced chiaroscuro, an easy but obvious and essentially unrealistic method of producing a three-dimensional effect: he had then to rely on tonal contrasts alone. Although the Impressionists were prestidigitorial in their solution of the problem, a feeling of dissatisfaction remained, and was only finally resolved by Cézanne after a lifetime of struggle. Cézanne's mature method was to "model" the actual pigment by brush strokes which take the form of planes so organized in block-like shapes that the pattern they make "seems" solid. These shapes are often reinforced by lines or hard edges, until the composition has the appearance of a hewn-out quarry, or, more positively, one of those Egyptian or Indian temples hewn out of a rocky mountain. Hence the familiar description of Cézanne's style as "sculptural."

Matisse's debt to Cézanne has never been in question: "Cézanne was the master of us all," he used to say. In 1899, perhaps incited by Pissarro, he had bought the small *Three Bathers* from Vollard, and this painting hung in his studio until he gave it to the Musée de la Ville de Paris (Petit Palais) in 1936. In a letter to Raymond Escholier, director of the museum (and author of an intimate account of Matisse's development as an artist), Matisse wrote: [1]

"Allow me to tell you that this picture is of the first importance in the work of Cézanne *because it is a very solid very complete realization* of a composition that he carefully studied in various canvases, which, though now in important collections, are not the studies that culminated in the present work.

"I have owned this canvas for thirty-seven years and I know it fairly well, I hope, though not entirely; it has sustained me spiritually in the critical moments of my career as an artist; I have drawn from it my faith and my perseverance: for this reason allow me to request that it be placed so that it may be seen to the best advantage. For this it needs both light and perspective. It is rich in color and surface and only when it is seen at a distance is it possible to appreciate the sweep of its lines and the exceptional sobriety of its relationships."

At the same time, and as part of the same deal with Vollard, Matisse acquired a plaster bust of Henri Rochefort by Rodin which he had seen at Vollard's. This work may not be very significant in relation to Matisse's own sculpture, but what is significant is that it was in this same year, 1899, that Matisse made his first experiment in sculpture. This was a "free copy of a piece by A. L. Barye, a bronze representing a *Jaguar Devouring a Hare*." Barr describes the extraordinary persistency with which Matisse worked on this piece: "For many months during 1900 he worked at night at the Ecole de la Ville de Paris on the rue Etienne Marcel, a free municipal school with a studio for sculpture. Even during the period of his exhausting labor on decorations for the Grand Palais he would work from eight to ten in the evening on his Barye copy. With characteristic thoroughness he even got the body of a cat from a medical school and dissected it to study the muscles of the back and claws. The planes of muscular structure he simplified somewhat but without loss of power and tension. The

93

1. Alfred H. Barr, Jr., *Matisse: His Art and His Public* (New York: Museum of Modern Art, 1951) p. 40 (my italics). Another translation is given in Raymond Escholier, *Matisse from the Life*, trans. Geraldine and H. M. Colville (London: Faber and Faber, 1960), p. 48.

Jaguar in its final state is a powerful interpretation of, and a magnificent homage to, Barye's masterpiece." [2]

We should perhaps now ask why a painter like Matisse, like Degas before him and Picasso after him, should turn with such absorption to the art of sculpture. Granted, as I have already said, that both arts are concerned with plasticity as a quality to be rendered, is it likely that an attack on the problem in a medium such as bronze could help an artist whose chosen medium is paint? This is perhaps a rhetorical question which can be answered only by the artist concerned. But we may suppose that Matisse, in the spirit of Cézanne, determined to preserve the physical solidity of volumes which had been sacrificed by the Impressionists. To this end, any research that led to an understanding of volume in relation to space was essential. In this connection the story of Matisse's only direct contact with Rodin is illuminating. It was first related by André Gide in his *Journal*, but Escholier gives Matisse's own version of the story: [3]

"I was taken to Rodin's studio in the rue de l'Université, by one of his pupils who wanted to show my drawings to his master. Rodin, who received me kindly, was only moderately interested. He told me I had 'facility of hand,' which wasn't true. He advised me to do detailed drawings and show them to him. I never went back. Understanding my direction, I thought I had need of someone's help to arrive at the right kind of detailed drawings. Because, if I could get the simple things (which are so difficult) right, first, then I could go on to the complex details; I should have achieved what I was after: the realization of my own reactions.

"My work-discipline was already the reverse of Rodin's. But I did not realize it then, for I was quite modest, and each day brought its revelation.

"I could not understand how Rodin could work on his St. John by cutting off the hand and holding it on a peg; he worked on details holding it in his left hand, ... anyhow keeping it detached from the whole, then replacing it on the end of the arm; then he tried to find its direction in accord with his general movement.

"Already I could only envisage the general architecture of a work of mine, replacing explanatory details by a living and suggestive synthesis."

This last sentence gives the clue to Matisse's approach to sculpture, and, by implication, to his whole artistic method. Matisse's second piece of sculpture, *The Slave*, was a direct challenge to Rodin. It was begun in 1900 but was not finished until 1903. Its stance is exactly the same as Rodin's *St. John the Baptist* (1879), though it is less than half the size and avoids the problem of accommodating the arms. The contemporary oil sketches Matisse made of the same model, one a painting in which the figure is of approximately the same height as the bronze, show the arms hanging limply down the side of the trunk. The difference between the Rodin and the Matisse is almost entirely a difference of surface treatment, but of surface reflecting not merely the local muscular tensions, but the linked succession of light and shade over the whole area of the body—a total "adventure." Although, as I have said, plastic volume, together with the tension between such volume or mass and the surrounding space, is the distinctive aim of the art of sculpture, Matisse believed that it could best be indicated by a "sweep of lines" or, rather, since this phrase as applied to Cézanne's painting is hardly applicable to a piece of sculpture, by a glittering succession of integrated planes. Speaking of Maillol, whose work is the perfection of realized volume, Matisse once said that "Maillol's sculpture and my work in that line have nothing in common. We never speak on the subject. For we couldn't understand one another. Maillol, like the Antique masters, proceeds by volume; *I am concerned with arabesque* like the Renaissance artists; Maillol did not like risks and I was drawn to them. He did not like adventure." [4]

We do not know which Renaissance artists Matisse had in mind on this occasion, but probably Michelangelo for one; a plaster cast of his *Slave* appears in one of Matisse's paintings (*Checker Game and Piano Music*, 1923). Perhaps Donatello too, though I know of no mention of this *arabesque* sculpture by Matisse. What Matisse meant by *arabesque* is not in question: it is the *one* word that might be used, if one only were permitted, to describe his style. It implies, of course, a linear style related to Arabic or Islamic carving and calligraphy, which is essentially intricate, but the word has been used to describe the same features in art generally; for example, the *Shorter Oxford English Dictionary* refers to "the arabesques of Raphael and the Renascence, founded on Graeco-Roman work, including representations of living creatures," and even declares that "to this variety the term

96

9

59

2. Barr, *op. cit.*, p. 52.   3. Escholier, *op. cit.*, p. 138.   4. Escholier, *op. cit.*, p. 141 (my italics).

is now usually applied." We must in any event distinguish between the stylistic and the decorative use of the term. In a superficial sense Matisse was influenced by the decorative art that he saw and admired during his visits to Algeria in 1906 and to Morocco in the winters of 1911-12 and 1912-13. On all these occasions he acquired pottery and textiles decorated with *arabesques*, and often used them in his still lifes. But when we apply the word *arabesque* to his sculpture, we mean a formal quality independent of color, more related to the exquisite plasterwork of the synagogues in Toledo and other cities. Matisse may have seen similar plasterwork in the mosques at Biskra or Tangier. The comparison is valid, however, only to the extent that Matisse, in his bronzes, seeks always to preserve an animated surface, a surface that reflects the play of the muscular stresses underneath. This is part of the "living and suggestive synthesis," reinforcing "the general architecture" of the work.

97
96 98

99
104 110
97 98

Nevertheless, Matisse's next piece of sculpture, the *Madeleine*, which exists in two versions (the first completed before *The Slave* in 1901, and the second, two years later), does again evoke, in its sinuosity and interflowing rhythm, the word *arabesque*, and so do the next group of bronzes, made by Matisse between 1905 and 1907. These include a *Thorn-Extractor* and a *Woman Leaning on Her Hands*[5] (both small pieces), and a *Standing Nude*, and a *Decorative Figure* which are comparable in scale to the *Madeleine* and *The Slave*.

It was shortly after completing this group of bronzes that Mrs. Michael Stein made notes of the instructions Matisse gave his pupils in the *académie* that he had been persuaded to open early in 1908. These notes, which Alfred Barr published for the first time in his great work on Matisse, are of supreme importance for the understanding of the principles and the methods the artist had established for his own practice by the age of thirty-eight. Some of his remarks on the "study of the model" are applicable to sculpture no less than to painting, such as "Arms are like rolls of clay, but the forearms are also like cords, for they can be twisted"; or "This pelvis fits into the thighs and suggests an amphora. Fit your parts into one another and build up your figure as a carpenter does a house"; or, again, "You may consider this Negro model a cathedral, built up of parts which form a solid, noble, towering construction—and as a lobster, because of the shell-like, tense muscular parts which fit so accurately and evidently into one another, with joints only large enough to hold their bones. But from time to time it is very necessary for you to remember that he is a Negro and not lose him and yourself in your construction."

When it comes to sculpture (and here it is instructive to bear in mind an image of the pieces Matisse himself had just made), Matisse warns his students against having a preconceived theory or effect with which the model must be made to agree. "It must impress you, awaken in you an emotion, which in turn you seek to express. You must forget all your theories, all your ideas before the subject. What part of these is really your own will be expressed in your expression of the emotion awakened in you by the subject." Always there is an interaction between perception and conception, between the form perceived and the artist's language of form. But sculpture has its special qualities. "In addition to the sensations one derives from a drawing, a sculpture must invite us to handle it as an object; just so the sculptor must feel, in making it, the particular demands for volume and mass. *The smaller the bit of sculpture, the more the essentials of form must exist.*" [6]

I emphasize this last sentence because it applies with peculiar force to the three small bronzes of 1905 and 1906. The *Little Head* especially, which is only 3¾ inches high, has a quite extraordinary suggestion of vitality. The *Torso* and the *Woman Leaning on Her Hands* in their rhythmic vitality lead

104

directly to the larger pieces. The *Standing Nude* might be profitably contrasted with one of Maillol's small bronzes, though there is no relevant piece of the same or an earlier date. Maillol once quoted Matisse's description of the *Venus de Milo* as "a young girl who puts herself forward," and that was Maillol's idea; his figures assert a natural exuberance. But Matisse's *Standing Nude* is not exuberant in this sense; rather she expresses a natural lassitude, or the modesty of a young girl who exposes her body passively. There is no attempt at classical elegance: the arms hang limply against the thighs, the feet are disproportionately large. But the form is coherent, and one rhythm, from the coiled hair to the heavy feet, binds it in inexorable unity.

110

This subordination of natural elegance to expressive rhythm is still more evident in the *Decorative Figure* of the year 1908. It is not obvious why Matisse should use the word "decorative" to describe this piece, unless he implied that rhythm is itself a decorative element. It is certainly, in this example, *arabesque*: the body itself is serpentine, the arms and the crossed legs interweave like plaited coils.

5. See Drawing No. 140.   6. Barr, *op. cit.*, Appendix A, pp. 550-552.

The oversize head, the disproportionate hands and feet, seem to be more "expressionistic" than any of the paintings of this same year (which incidentally include a *Still Life* in the Yale University Art Gallery in which can be seen a plaster maquette for the *Standing Nude*), though the piece may be compared with the famous *Self Portrait* now in the Copenhagen Art Museum, originally acquired by Michael and Sarah Stein late in 1906. But by 1907 the expressionism of sculpture and painting begin to coincide: the *Blue Nude* (souvenir of Biskra) and the *Reclining Nude I*, which were both executed at 109 Collioure in the early months of 1907, are versions in the two media of an identical theme. Here, better than anywhere, we discern the intimate relationship between the two approaches to the problems of form. It is significant that the sculpture preceded the painting. According to Barr [7], "while modeling he wet the clay too freely so that when he turned the stand the figure fell off on its head and was ruined. Exasperated, he began to paint the figure instead." The painting then became a study for the sculpture and the result was the bronze we know, one of Matisse's masterpieces. As Alfred Barr says: "That Matisse himself found the *Reclining Nude* exceptionally interesting is proven 109 by the fact that for years after it was done, and far more often than any other piece of sculpture, he incorporated it as an important compositional element in his paintings." [8]

It should perhaps be noted that this was the year in which, according to Gertrude Stein [9], Matisse introduced Picasso to African sculpture—an event with immediate and far reaching effect on the future development of European art.

Matisse was now fully committed to an expressionist style in sculpture, and I would emphasize once again that it is in his modeled bronzes that he gives much the freest reign to this extreme in his style. Whether "expressionist" is the correct word to use to describe Matisse's style is perhaps an open question. "To dream, that is the whole thing, and to act with precision while dreaming," is Georges Duthuit's admirable definition of the style of Matisse, and in all this, he adds, "there is not a trace of expressionism... The spectacle is neither beautiful nor ugly; there is no spectacle, only a movement, an obstacle race whose goal is, in itself and projected outside itself, motion in liberty." [10] Nevertheless, there is in Matisse's work an element for which a psychological explanation is available, and it is the explanation that has been offered for expressionism in art. Alfred Barr, in one of his notes, mentions the researches of Ludwig Münz and Viktor Löwenfeld. [11] These researches show that in modeling clay the artist's hands unconsciously respond to "inner," somatic sensations; in the process of modeling the artist gives prominence to those details in his composition which correspond to "haptic" sensations. Such expressive emphasis is most evident in the modeling done by blind children, but it is not necessary to be blind to allow this emphasis to appear when the aim of the artist is "motion in liberty." This very freedom in the hand will be "expressive." Or, as Duthuit himself writes, "Painting will no longer be a *means of expression*, it will be *expression* or rather, expression and means will be one and the same thing." [12]. This is equally true of sculpture.

Matisse now approached his most monumental task in sculpture. There was some early confusion in the dating of the series of four large *Bas Reliefs* commonly known as *The Backs* [13]. The Matisse 135 – 138 family now dates the first version 1909, which places it in the midst of the remarkable outburst of sculptural activity of the years 1908-1911. It began quietly enough with the *Two Negresses* and 111 *Seated Figure, Right Hand on Ground*, which were notable for their uncompromising plasticity; no concession is made to the inherent qualities of the metal: they are direct reproductions of fingered clay. Then comes *La Serpentine*, so radical a departure from the classical tradition to which the subject 113 and pose relate it that it was at first regarded as a caricature, but is now seen as a decisive "happening" in the history of modern sculpture. But it merely transposes into sculpture the rhythmic inventions that Matisse had made in the same year in his famous paintings of the *Dance*. It is true that the *Dance* represents, more than any other work of Matisse's, "motion in liberty," and that *La Serpentine* represents on the contrary a figure in languid repose; it is also true that the bodies of dancers in the painting are of natural proportions whereas the body of *La Serpentine* has calves thicker than thighs and thighs thicker than the trunk. Nevertheless, the rhythmical intention is the same: to "thin" and compose the forms "so that the movement would be completely comprehensible from all points

7. Barr, *op. cit.*, p. 94.   8. *Ibid.*, p. 100.
9. Gertrude Stein, *The Autobiography of Alice B. Toklas* (New York: Harcourt, Brace & Co., 1933), pp. 77-78.
10. Georges Duthuit, *The Fauvist Painters*, trans. Ralph Manheim (New York: Wittenborn, Schulz, 1950), p. 93.

11. Ludwig Münz and Viktor Löwenfeld, *Die Plastischen Arbeiten Blinder* (Brunn, 1934).
Viktor Löwenfeld, *The Nature of Creative Activity* (London, 1939).
12. Duthuit, *op. cit.*, p. 62 (Duthuit's italics).
13. See Drawing No. 170.

of view." I believe that the distortions can be explained by the haptic theory already mentioned; but everything is subordinated to the rhythmic movement.

116   117   The *Five Heads of Jeannette* represent progressive stages in significant deformation. *Jeannettes I* and *II* are "realistic," though *II* shows a general softening of the features (eyebrows, eyelids, and hair). *Jean-*
118   *nette III* is already decisively stylized: the hair broken into "knobs," the eyes enlarged and protruded, the cheekbones heightened, the nose made prominent; it is also twice the size of the preceding busts.
119   120   In *IV* and *V* all these tendencies are progressively enhanced: the hair gradually reduced to one "hank," the eyes in their bony sockets greatly enlarged, all the planes simplified and given the power of a mechanical thrust.

135 – 138   Before discussing the significance of this "progressive deformation," we should look at the comparable evolution of the *Bas Reliefs (The Backs)*. These reliefs, each approximately 74 inches high, represent four progressive simplifications of the same theme—the back of a nude woman seen against a wall. There is an interval of more than twenty years between the first treatment and the final one (1930). *II* is definitely dated 1913, and was not cast until 1956. *III* is dated 1916-17, and *IV* remained unexhibited until after the death of Matisse. The series of four *Bas Reliefs* was first shown together at the Henri Matisse Retrospective Exhibition in Paris in 1956. [14]

"Deformation" is perhaps not the right word to use in describing the progressive stages of Matisse's treatment of this motive. What is involved is again a process of simplification and concentration, each version becoming more powerful in its impact. Significant is the introduction in *Bas Relief III* of long, falling hair which merges with the head. In the final version it is seen to be an essential counterthrust to the upraised shoulders and arm. The combined effect of the four *Bas Reliefs* when exhibited side by side is as powerful as anything in the whole range of modern sculpture.

122   The last considerable group of sculpture (apart from a bronze *Head of Marguerite*, 1915-16, and
125   three minor bronzes of 1918) was produced in the years 1925-1930. It begins with the *Large Seated Nude* of 1925, one of Matisse's finest bronzes. It is closely related to the oil painting of the *Odalisque*
166   168   *with Raised Arms* of 1923 (Chester Dale Collection) and two lithographs, *Seated Nude with Arms Raised*, of 1924 and 1925. (Two charcoal drawings of the same subject also exist.) [15] Once again we see how the technique of modeling imposes a certain simplification and even geometrization on the artist; it looks as though the final planes had been shaved off by a knife. The painted nude leans against an armchair; the bronze nude leans against nothing and seems to be precariously balanced on a round tuffet. As Alfred Barr remarks, it would have been easy for the sculptor to have corrected this lack of balance; but it seems to me that his intention was to isolate the body so that the spectator can better appreciate the formal *arabesque* of the "pose". The same formal *arabesque* is further deve-
128   130   loped in *Reclining Nude II* of 1927-1929 and *III* of 1929, which are sequential to the *Reclining Nude I* of 1907 already discussed. That Matisse should have taken up this same theme after twenty years shows that it held some special fascination for him, and again one resorts to the ambiguous word *arabesque*. It is an *arabesque* movement of interflowing limbs and torso, an anticipation of Henry Moore's extensive development of the same motif. There is also an emanation from these figures of that feeling of languor and bodily ease which, as we know from various statements he made, was one of Matisse's ideals in art.

131   133   The *Venus in a Shell*, of which two versions exist (1930 and 1932), belongs essentially to the same
127   group; it is a vertical exploitation of the same *arabesque*. Very different is the *Henriette, Second State* of 1927, which has the compactness and the dignity of a Roman sculptural portrait; it is a powerful work that does not seem to have much relation to the rest of Matisse's sculpture. Nor, for very
132   different reasons, does the *Tiari* of 1930 (done on his return from a voyage to Tahiti). The "tiari" from which the piece takes its title is a large tropical flower Matisse had seen on his travels, but it is
119   transformed into a female head, not so very different from *Jeannette IV* in its general configuration, yet carried to a degree of fantasy very rare in Matisse's work. There are three versions of the *Tiari*, one with a necklace.
134   The only remaining piece of sculpture made by Matisse in his lifetime is the *Christ* for the altar of the Chapel at Vence as part of a complete décor (his designs were finished early in 1950). He is said to have studied the Christian iconography of the subject before attempting this particular task, but in the end the design was original enough, though not unlike the attenuated bronze figures

---

14. This information has been obtained from Marguerite Duthuit and Jean Matisse, based on their comprehensive files from the casting establishment, and on their own complete files of exhibitions.

15. See Painting No. 63.

of Christ found in West German bronze sculpture and enamels of the eleventh and twelfth centuries. It takes an appropriate place in the general decoration of the Chapel, but is not in itself a characteristic example of Matisse's sculpture.

An important part was played by Matisse's sculpture in his total *œuvre*. It has been asked whether Matisse made a very significant contribution to the development of modern sculpture as a whole. It is difficult to detect any influence of his work on his contemporaries or followers which could not as reasonably be attributed to Degas, Rodin, or Maillol, yet Matisse was perhaps the first sculptor to use the expressive deformations that have become so characteristic of sculpture in the past fifty years. But this aspect of his work has found its detractors. For example, Jean Selz accuses Matisse of not being quite certain of his intentions: "He seems to waver between an impressionistic modeling, resembling that of Bonnard's few little sculptures, and a style of distortion rather like that of Picasso." What I have described as "progressive stages in significant deformation" in the five *Heads of Jeannette*, Selz sees as signs of uncertainty or hesitation. Many of Matisse's smaller figures, and especially his nudes, Selz writes, "are marred by an uncouth flabbiness which is not counter-balanced by the charm of a deliberately rudimentary modeling technique. The play of volumes and planes lacks that balance, or calculated imbalance, which is the mark of a really great sculptor." He even accuses Matisse of an "obvious lack of sensuality." [16]

It will be seen from what I have written above that I cannot agree with these opinions. The "distortion" criticized by Selz is an intentional device, as I have explained, and the imbalance is certainly calculated. What Selz calls "uncouth flabbiness" is presumably the quality of "relaxation" which again was a deliberate aim of Matisse's— "an art of balance, of purity and serenity devoid of troubling or depressing subject-matter." It is true that Matisse's sculpture does not have the same "grace" or "lucidity" as his paintings, but this again was deliberate. "Charm, lightness, crispness," he wrote, "all these are passing sensations. I have a canvas on which the colors are still fresh and I begin work on it again. The colors will probably grow heavier—the freshness of the original tones *will give way to greater solidity, an improvement to my mind, but less seductive to the eye*." [17] To carry that "improvement" still farther Matisse resorted to the art of sculpture, the art of greater solidity.

16. Jean Selz, *Modern Sculpture, Origins and Evolutions*, trans. by Annette Michelson (London: Heinemann, 1963) pp. 189, 192.

17. Barr, *op.cit.*, pp. 119-123, Henri Matisse (my italics), "Notes of a Painter", originally published *La Grande Revue* (Paris, Dec. 25, 1908).

William S. Lieberman # NOTES ON MATISSE AS A DRAFTSMAN

It is difficult to write again concerning the graphic art of Matisse. Elsewhere, and more than once, I have analyzed his production as a printmaker as well as an illustrator of books. A discussion of his drawings might await a separate publication. But I realize now that the most informative, certainly the most eloquent, remarks concerning his graphic art are those by Matisse himself.

Four such statements are reprinted by Alfred Barr in the definitive monograph *Matisse: His Art and His Public*. They should be read, I would recommend, in the following order. First, a letter of 1947 to Henry Clifford[1] upon the occasion of the artist's retrospective at the Philadelphia Museum. The essay is called *Exactitude is Not Truth*[2] and Matisse talks of his draftsmanship, in particular a succession of self portraits of 1939. Second, an earlier and more programmatic dictum, *Notes of a Painter*[3], that originally appeared in *La Grande Revue* in 1908. Third, a similar but less formal statement, also of 1908, that compiles remarks addressed by Matisse to his students. These observations were recorded by an American, Mrs. Michael Stein, when she audited Matisse's classes at a school established (with her support) in a deconsecrated convent on the rue de Sèvres. Mrs. Stein's record was edited and annotated by Alfred Barr as *A Great Artist Speaks to His Students*[4]. Fourth, Matisse's explanation of his illustrated books and the aesthetic which dominated the production of the best of them, *How I Made My Books*,[5] first published in 1946.

No matter how brief, any bibliography is a boring introduction to an essay and I must apologize. But Matisse's own writings are important not only to students of his art but to anyone concerned with visual perception. His assertions are authentic, they are vivid and consistent, they ring with truth and clarity. In conversation he could be equally eloquent. In 1948 he told me: "My drawing is the most direct and purest translation of my emotion. This is made possible by simplification of media. I have the feeling that my emotion expresses itself through the medium of plastic writing. As soon as my line—inspired, so to speak, with a life of its own—has molded the light of the empty sheet without destroying the tender whiteness of the paper, I stop. I can no longer add or change. The page is written, no correction is possible."

In painting, Matisse surely is the greatest colorist of our time. The essence of his art, however, lies in the rhythm of his line. He was a master draftsman and drawing occupied him constantly and compulsively. His interest in printmaking was less sustained, concentrated into relatively short intervals throughout his career. During the final quarter-century of his life, the majority of his prints consist of illustrations to some of the most beautifully designed books ever manufactured.

As a graphic artist how does he differ from his contemporaries of the School of Paris? Bonnard and Vuillard both produced many prints, particularly lithographs, but few of their drawings are memorable. Rouault, Matisse's oldest friend, and Villon are among the foremost printmakers of our century; indeed their achievement as engravers is perhaps more important than as painters, but who recalls easily a drawing in black and white by either painter? Dufy worked in woodcut, etching and lithography and was as well a prolific draftsman, but the very facility of his calligraphy conspires to obscure its refinement. The single painter of the School of Paris who as a graphic artist— as a draftsman, a printmaker, and an illustrator—demands comparison with Matisse remains, inevitably, Picasso.

1. Not the same letter reproduced herein, p. 7.
2. Barr, *op. cit.*, p. 561.
3. Barr, *op. cit.*, pp. 119-123.
4. Barr, *op. cit.*, pp. 550-552.
5. Barr, *op. cit.*, p. 563.

How often Matisse and Picasso are thrust together! This was a rivalry in which neither deliberately participated, but which occurs again and again at specific moments—their individual relationships to the individual Steins, the painting of *La Joie de Vivre* [6] and *Les Demoiselles d'Avignon*, commissions received by each for illustrated books, even exhibitions in France and abroad.

Two stories illustrate Picasso's attitude toward Matisse. Shortly after Matisse's death James Soby visited Picasso. After a procession of canvases—in Picasso's studio always a choreographed production— Soby observed that one of the paintings resembled a Matisse. Picasso, seldom taken aback, paused and then replied, "Now I must paint for us both." A few years earlier I had presented Picasso with a copy of Alfred Barr's monograph on Matisse. Picasso accepted the volume, weighed it in one hand and somewhat peevishly remarked that it was much heavier than Barr's monograph on himself.

Picasso, in his graphic art, creates a world apart from his painting. He works on paper at night. He returns to specific subjects—for instance the artist as a hero—and both his drawings and prints offer a narrative continuity which his paintings usually lack. Picasso, in addition, is frequently concerned with allegory and, during the last two decades, his graphic work has become increasingly autobiographical.

Matisse always drew from the model and his subjects, most often, are set in his studio. His interest was form rather than content and frequently, indeed obsessively, he developed successive variations on a single theme. Each sheet presents a different attitude, another view or nuance. Matisse himself described such series as "a motion picture film of the feelings of an artist."

His earliest drawings after plaster casts are competent renditions in charcoal. But as early as 1900 his studies of a bearded male model, sometimes called *The Slave*, already define the essential characteristic of his draftsmanship—a sure handwriting which unifies decorative design and expressionist distortion. Elegance sometimes conceals the boldness of his compositions, for instance in the detailed pencil studies of 1919 devoted to a model in a *Plumed Hat*. With brush or pen and ink, Matisse's line is freer and often more economical. His later drawings in charcoal are frequently concerned with spatial relationships and the atmospheric play of shade and light. Matisse's drawing and prints, unlike those of Picasso, are almost always in black and white.

9   96

163 - 165

In later life, Matisse himself considered his most important series of drawings those gathered together and reproduced as *Dessins: Thèmes et Variations* published in 1943 with a preface by Aragon. The portfolio contains 170 drawings of 1941 and 1942 divided into seventeen sequences or themes, each containing from three to eighteen variations. Matisse wrote to his son Pierre, "For a year now I have been making an enormous effort in drawing. I say effort but that is a mistake, because what has occurred is a *floraison* after fifty years of effort."

195 - 201

Taken individually Matisse's appreciation of these drawings seems somewhat exaggerated. However, he attached great significance to the series, and in 1948 he distributed separate sequences to various provincial museums in France.

His last major series of drawings, the free working studies, for the decoration of the Chapel at Vence, assume mural proportions. Matisse was already an invalid, and many of them were drawn with a stick almost twice his height. In their final version, as installed in the church, they offer a stunning background in black on white upon which play the splendid colors of the stained glass windows he himself designed.

219

Unlike Picasso, Matisse never maintained a continuous interest in printmaking, nor was he in any sense a technical innovator. Matisse's accomplishment as an etcher and lithographer was, nevertheless, prodigious. In the making of prints he sought and found refreshment from easel painting, but his interest was sporadic and incidental to his production as a painter.

222   223
225
234 - 237

Matisse first worked on copper in 1903. These early drypoints are frankly exercises, the most assured of which, *Self Portrait*, offers a factual reflection of the artist's image at the age of thirty-three. In 1906 Matisse composed his first lithographs and carved his only three woodcuts. With one exception—a sketch of the church and harbor of Collioure—the subjects are studies of women, heads, or full figures drawn standing, sitting and crouching. The poses seem strained, even distorted, and this series of a dozen lithographs relates closely to his sculpture of the same time. After a lapse of several years, in 1914, Matisse resumed printmaking and produced nine or ten lithographs, at

6. See Drawing No. 143.

least fourteen monotypes and some fifty etchings. This second series of lithographs seems somewhat more refined than those of 1906. The designs are free, large, and the attitudes softer. The placement of the figure in relation to the printed sheet is always arresting, while details of the torso are isolated and swept into the sensual rhythm of Matisse's line.

The monotypes offer a wider variety of subjects including—in addition to nudes—portraits, still lives and interior scenes. One may be a self portrait; meticulously printed, probably from copper plates, each is of course unique. Matisse is quoted as having been "very much pleased with those prints of his of white lines on a black background."

The etchings of the same year are more intimate than either the lithographs or the monotypes. Mostly portraits of friends and family, they build a brilliant sequence of quick and informal characterizations: the wives of the painters Galanis and Gris, Mme Vignier and her daughter Irène, Yvonne Landsberg, the artist's wife and children, and—surprising to a student of Matisse's art—a number of men, among them the Spaniards Massia, Iturrino and Olivares, the British museologist Matthew Stewart Pritchard and the American painter Walter Pach. Only one professional model seems to have posed, "Loulou", who appears head, front and back. As portraits these etchings, like several of Matisse's drawings, offer much more penetrating characterizations than do any of his paintings where portraiture usually surrenders to decorative effect.

The portraits were finished with astonishing speed after careful consideration of the sitter. The drawing is quick and decisive. Like all of Matisse's etchings, each is distinguished by its simplicity. Individual features are reduced to vivid details, and often the contours of the face fill the rectangular frame of the copper plate. The figure is treated at greater length only occasionally. Several friends, for instance Josette Gris, sat more than once, and in the series there are as many as seven different likenesses of the same individual. Matisse had originally intended to gather the portraits as an album; but, instead, the etchings were issued separately in editions of five to fifteen proofs each. To this gallery of miniatures he added a few studies of the nude and a sketch of foliage.

During the next decade Matisse etched a few plates, but not until 1922 does he seem to have returned to working on stone. He began with some hesitation, but then in 1925 alone he printed more than twenty lithographs. The most notable is a progression of seated figures which reaches a climax in two large versions of a nude in an armchair and culminates in the voluptuous *Odalisque in Striped Pantaloons*.

277 - 281
293

Between 1926 and 1930 the painter increased his annual manufacture of lithographs. In the two earlier series of lithographs of 1906 and 1914, Matisse had developed a linear style quite independent from his drawings in charcoal or in pen and ink. The lithographs of the late 1920's, however, are simply drawings transferred to stone. The subjects of some sixty prints are models, nude or draped. They appear singly, surrounded by flowers, fabrics, and furniture. Matisse's drawing varies from spontaneous studies in line to strongly modeled, meticulous delineations. Sometimes the pose is conventional, sometimes radically contorted. In 1927 the subject is frequently a ballet dancer, perhaps inspired by his association with Diaghilev. Occasionally the model is viewed from above, and the arabesques formed by the accessories and figure merge into one fluid pattern.

303   306   308

Suddenly, at the end of the twenties, Matisse resumed etching. Within a few months he produced a constellation of about 125 plates, studies of nudes and odalisques, and a series of girls gazing at goldfish. Again, as in 1914, Matisse worked directly on the plate from the model. Sometimes, like the lithographs, the etchings repeat or anticipate motifs in his painting. Usually, although often similar in subject, they remain distinct.

At first this series of etchings may seem incidental, but, freshly examined, it reduces daring syncopations of a pose or movement into essential lines. Matisse plays endless variations on the same themes. The concise reductions of the etchings of 1929 dispel the still and heavy atmosphere of the seraglio which permeates the lithographs of the late twenties. Matisse's line is lively and inquisitive as it dances out the tensions and balances that sustain the series.

During the thirties Matisse continued to make a few etchings and lithographs each year, but as a printmaker he never again attained the concentrated and prolific production of 1914 and the late twenties. By 1935 he had produced some 200 intaglio plates, almost 150 lithographs as well as the few woodcuts and monotypes.

During the last years of his life, he found time to complete two separate series of independent prints quite different in media and style from any of his previous graphic work. The first consists of about two dozen linoleum cuts—heads of women and still lifes of fruit—unexpectedly angular in style and cut between 1941 and 1950. The second series, now dated 1948, are freely brushed aquatints which, when printed, create the effect of bold and simple drawings in ink.

Curiously, Matisse—the consummate colorist—in his prints and drawings almost never worked in color. He remained faithful to the tradition of black and white. He distilled and elaborated themes in which he had been working as a painter and sculptor. In his painting the colors are not inherently sensuous, as has been so often remarked. The tactile values are created by the rhythm of his line which strengthens the painted forms as well as the colors they contain. These lines appear in their quintessence in Matisse's drawings and prints.

After 1930 Matisse's principal energies as a printmaker were devoted to the illustration of books whose poems offered fresh inspiration and expanded the iconography of his art. Strangely, he had received only one commission from Ambroise Vollard, the great French publisher— a single etching for a projected album of nudes by several artists.

It was the courageous Swiss publisher Albert Skira who, in 1932, launched Matisse in his tardy debut as an illustrator. The previous year Skira had presented Picasso's etchings for Ovid's *Metamorphoses*. Skira's second volume was to be equally distinguished, Matisse's etchings for the poems of Mallarmé.

Anyone interested in these illustrations must ideally study the maquette of the volume which was presented to the Baltimore Museum of Art with the Cone Collection. It contains much more than the twenty-nine illustrations finally published; Baltimore is fortunate to possess many additional plates as well as the complete series of working drawings. When composing illustrations for any of his books, Matisse liked to begin with the poems already set in handsome type and printed on handsome paper. He also liked plenty of empty pages on which he could draw. On each page of the Cone copy of the Mallarmé, one sees Matisse at work. The final illustrations, with their deceptive effect of effortless spontaneity, evoke a specific title or phrase. Only after many essays was Matisse satisfied with their continuity and fitness to the poems. "This is the work I have completed after reading Mallarmé with pleasure... The drawing is not massed toward the center as usual but spreads across the entire page. The problem was to balance each pair of facing pages—the one with etching white, the other with the typography relatively black. I achieved this by modifying my arabesques in such a way that the spectator's attention would be interested as much by the entire page as by the promise of reading the text."

After a series of major operations left Matisse an invalid in 1941, he devoted a great part of his time to book illustration. The creation of lavishly illustrated books was an endeavor admirably suited to his last years. During his increasingly prolonged confinements in bed at Nice, Vence, Paris, and then Nice again, he could easily spread before him the materials and texts for his projects. Illustration naturally demanded less physical exertion than painting.

Pasiphaé-Chant de Minos, extracts from de Montherlant's *Les Crétois*, with linoleum cuts by Matisse was published in 1941. These blocks, however, differ radically from the woodcuts of 1906. Instead of carving away to achieve a design in relief which prints in black, Matisse retained most of the linoleum's surface. The solid black rectangle of the uncut surface serves as a background to the engraved compositon it contains. When inked, the incised line of the design prints as white.

Matisse cautions: "The lino should not be used as a cheap substitute for wood, because it gives to a print its own special character, quite different from woodcut, and therefore should be studied. The gouge is controlled directly by the sensibility of the engraver. Indeed this is so true that the least distraction during the execution of a line causes a slight pressure of the fingers on the gouge and influences the drawing for the worse. Engraving on the linoleum is a true medium for the painter illustrator."

The last three significant series of book illustrations by Matisse are *Jazz, Florilège des Amours de Ronsard* and *Poèmes de Charles d'Orléans* published between 1947 and 1950.

At the age of seventy-five, during a twelve-month confinement to his bed, Matisse composed *Jazz*. The title itself evolved from the affinity Matisse felt between his own method of improvisation and that of jazz musicians. Actually, most of the scenes of *Jazz* are taken from circus life and represent sword swallowers, knife throwers, cowboys and tank swimmers. Several of the performers existed in life, for instance Codomas and Monsieur Loyal, a famous clown.

The illustrations for *Jazz* were not conceived as original prints. Instead, they are splendid color reproductions of the signs Matisse worked out with scissors, paste and pins. The artist first covered large sheets of white paper with thin washes of brilliant colors. From these he cut out figures and forms which he then arranged with paste and pins into bold patterns. These collages of painted pieces of paper (Matisse called them "drawings with scissors") were reproduced by *pochoir* (stencil) using the same colors Matisse himself had originally mixed.

Jazz was published in two editions, a book with a text and as an album of twenty plates. In the book five or six pages of text are placed before each stencil. The text, by Matisse himself and in his handwriting, has not yet been translated into English. It discusses not only drawing and art in general but contains many short and quasi-philosophical reflections on such diverse subjects as flower arrangements, airplanes, belief in God, hatred, love, happiness and future life. "I can offer some remarks, notes made in the course of my lifetime as a painter. I ask of those who have the patience to read them that indulgence which is generally accorded to the writing of painters." Visually, the chief purposes of the passages of text is relief between the dazzling, brightly colored composition of the plates.

The love lavished upon the *Ronsard* is apparent as one turns its pages. The format is large and handsome. To his own choice of poems Matisse drew one hundred and twenty-six lithographs printed in brown on an off-white paper. In this volume, unlike the Mallarmé or the Montherlant, Matisse does not stress the left-hand right-hand balance between text and illustration. The two are composed together. A scene of a woman bathing under a willow covers an entire folio; a pattern of leaves lightly embroiders a double spread of pages; heads, fragments of a nude, flowers, fruit, decorate other pages of poems, larger full-page illustrations suggest in a few sure lines scenes of pastoral romance, the reverberations of a kiss, the silhouette of a vase, the song of birds. The conception of each page is fresh and unexpected, as lyric and graceful as the poems themselves.

After this tribute to Ronsard, Matisse made an elaborate bow to another poet, Charles d'Orléans. In a large notebook of a hundred pages Matisse penned forty poems and ornamented the manuscript with colored crayons. As an introduction, the first four pages are covered with fleurs-de-lis, the royal emblem of France chosen by Charles' grandfather. A gay title page in blue and red faces a noble profile portrait of the author. The fleurs-de-lis motive is thereafter repeated on each left-hand page. The lilies of France vary in size, number and arrangement. The leaves themselves are drawn in two colors, the combination changing with each page. Opposite these fields appear the various rondels, ballads and songs. On the right-hand pages Matisse copied the courtly verses in pen and ink and framed each poem with a witty rococo border. Five times the pages are interrupted by illustrations—three portraits of women, a meadow of rabbits, and a nude enshrined in a flower. It is impossible not to share Matisse's light-hearted pleasure in the creation of this book. He delights in teasing his ingenuity as far as possible within the arbitrary limits of the fleurs-de-lis foliates. The brightly colored illuminations are elegant, playful, and extravagant.

A half century ago Matisse was interviewed by an American lady, and his remarks addressed to "the American people" I find not inappropriate here.

It was the spring of 1913, the time of the Armory show, and Miss Clara T. MacChesney visited Matisse at Issy-les-Moulineaux. She expected "a long-haired, slovenly dressed, eccentric man." She was disappointed and said so. She quite frankly did not admire "a huge, gaudy-hued canvas" and asked, "Do you recognize harmony of color?"

Matisse, almost with indignation, replied: "I certainly do think of harmony of color, and of composition, too. Drawing is for me the art of being able to express myself with line. When an artist or student draws a nude figure with painstaking care, the result is drawing, and not emotion.

"I never use pastels or watercolors, and I only make studies from models, not to use in a picture—*mais pour me nourrir*—to strengthen my knowledge; and I never work from a previous sketch or study. I now draw with feeling, and not anatomically." Matisse added, parenthetically, "I know how to draw 'correctly,' having studied form for so long."

Matisse concluded: "Oh, do tell the American people that I am a normal man; that I am a devoted husband and father, that I have three fine children, that I go to the theatre, ride horseback, have a comfortable home, a fine garden, that I love flowers, just like any man."

PAINTINGS

1   Books and Candle   1890
Nature morte aux livres
15 × 18⅛″
Jean Matisse, Paris

Interior with a Top Hat   (1896)
Intérieur au chapeau
31½×37⅜″
Monsieur and Madame Georges Duthuit, Paris

3   Still Life   (1896)
Nature morte à l'auto-portrait
25 ½ × 32″
Sam Salz, New York

5   Courtyard of a Farm
in Brittany   1897
Cour de ferme bretonne
12¾ × 16″
Private Collection, Paris

6   Still Life   (1898)
Nature morte
15 × 18″
Private Collection, Paris

4   Breton Serving Girl   (1896)
La desserte
35 ½ × 29 ½″
Private Collection, Paris

Interior: Sideboard and Table   (1899)
Nature morte: buffet et table
25 ½ × 32 ½″
Mrs. Robert Woods Bliss, Washington, D.C.

7   Peach Trees in Bloom   1899
Les pêchers en fleur
13¹/₂ × 18¹/₄″
Private collection, Paris

12   Japanese Lady (Madame Matisse)   (1901)
La Japonaise
46×31½″
Private Collection, Paris

10   Self Portrait   (1900)
Auto-portrait
$25\,^3/_{16} \times 17\,^3/_4''$
Monsieur and Madame Georges Duthuit, Paris

9   Male Model   (1900)
Le serf
39⅜×28¾″
Mr. and Mrs. Pierre Matisse

13   Standing Nude   (1901)
      Nu debout
      31½×23¼″
      Mr. and Mrs. Gifford Phillips, Santa Monica, California

11   The Seine   (1900-01)
La Seine
23×28″
Wright Saltus Ludington, Santa Barbara, California

14   A Glimpse of Notre Dame in the Late Afternoon   1902
Notre-Dame, une fin d'après-midi
$28\frac{1}{2} \times 21\frac{1}{2}''$
Albright-Knox Art Gallery, Buffalo, New York, Seymour H. Knox Fund

15   Guitarist (Madame Matisse)   (1903)
Guitariste
21 ½ × 15″
Mr. and Mrs. Ralph F. Colin, New York

16   Carmelina   (1903)
$32 \times 23\frac{1}{2}''$
Museum of Fine Arts, Boston

St. Anne's Chapel   (1904)
La Chapelle Sainte-Anne
23⅝×28¾″
Mr. and Mrs. Pierre Matisse

18   Woman with the Hat   (1904-05)
Femme au chapeau; Madame Matisse
$32 \times 23\frac{1}{2}''$
Mr. and Mrs. Walter A. Haas, San Francisco

Woman with Parasol   (1905)
Femme à l'ombrelle
18¹/₁₆ × 14³/₄″
Musée Matisse, Cimiez-Nice

20   The Port of Abaill, Collioure   (1905)
Le Port d'Abaill,
$23\frac{5}{8} \times 58\frac{1}{4}''$
Jean Matisse, Paris

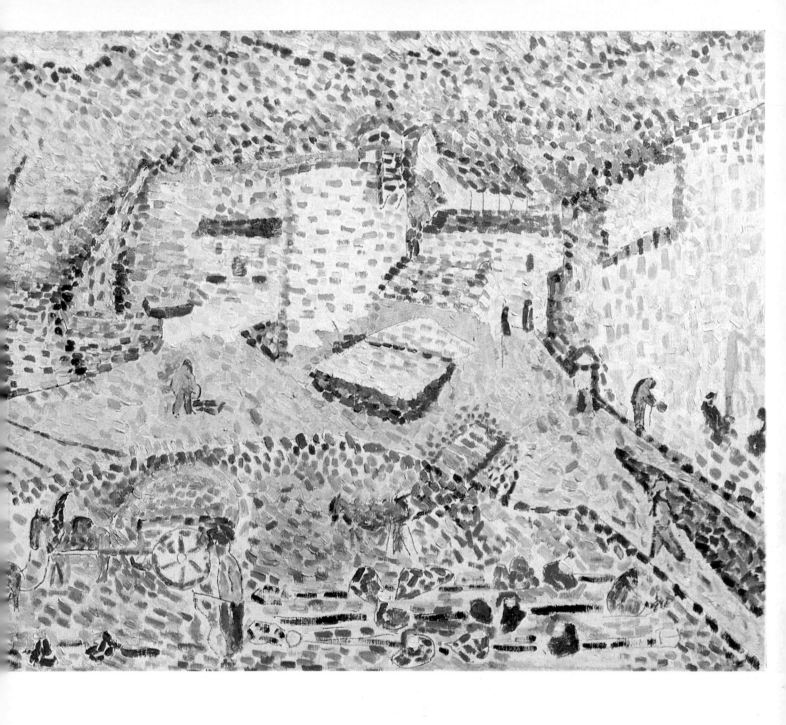

22   Reading   (1906)
La lecture
29½ × 24½″
Mr. and Mrs. William Goetz, Los Angeles

Pastoral   (1906)
Pastorale
18 1/8 × 21 3/4 ″
Musée d'Art Moderne de la Ville de Paris

23   Still Life with Geranium Plant and Fruit   (1906)
Nature morte au géranium
38½ × 31½″
The Art Institute of Chicago, The Joseph Winterbotham Collection

The Young Sailor, II   1906
Jeune marin à la casquette
39⅜ × 31⅞″
Mr. and Mrs. Leigh B. Block, Chicago

25   Music (sketch)   (1907)
La musique (esquisse)
29×24″
The Museum of Modern Art, New York, gift of A. Conger Goodyear in honor of Alfred H. Barr, Jr.

Bathers with a Turtle   1908
Baigneuses à la tortue
70½×86¾″
City Art Museum of Saint Louis, gift of Mr. and Mrs. Joseph Pulitzer, Jr.

27   Girl with Green Eyes   (1909)
La femme aux yeux verts
26 × 20″
The San Francisco Museum of Art, bequest of Harriet Lane Levy

28   Pierre Matisse   (1909)
16 × 13″
Private Collection, New York

29   Dance (first version)   (1909)
La danse — esquisse
102½ × 153½″
The Museum of Modern Art, New York,
gift of Nelson A. Rockefeller in honor of
Alfred H. Barr, Jr.   Pages 58-59

30   Girl with a Black Cat (Marguerite Matisse)   (1910)
Jeune fille au chat noir (Marguerite Matisse)
37 × 25¼″
Monsieur and Madame Georges Duthuit, Paris

31   The Blue Window   (1911)
        La fenêtre bleue
        51 ½ × 35 ⅝″
        The Museum of Modern Art, New York, Abby Aldrich Rockefeller Fund

32   Zorah in Yellow   (1912)
La robe jaune
32×25″
Mr. and Mrs. Alfred Cowles, Lake Forest, Illinois

Oranges (Tangier)   (1912)
Nature morte aux oranges
37×33⅛″
Monsieur and Madame Pablo Picasso, Mougins, France

34   Open Window, Tangier   (1913)
La fenêtre ouverte, Tanger
59½×37″
Private Collection, Paris

35   Mademoiselle Yvonne Landsberg   1914
58 × 38½"
The Philadelphia Museum of Art,
The Louise and Walter Arensberg Collection

36   The Open Window, Collioure   (1914)
La porte-fenêtre
46×35½″
Monsieur and Madame Georges Duthuit, Paris

38   Lilac Branch   (1914)
      La branche de lilas
      57 × 38″
      Private Collection, New York

37   View of Notre Dame   (1914)
Une vue de Notre-Dame
57¾×37″
Private Collection, New York

Tree Near Trivaux Pond   (1916-17)
Arbre près de l'étang de Trivaux
36½ × 29¼"
The Trustees of the Tate Gallery, London

39   Portrait of Madame Greta Prozor   (1916)
$57\frac{1}{2} \times 37\frac{3}{4}''$
Private Collection, New York

Lorette and Aicha   (1916)
15 18″
Private Collection, New York

44   The Green Gandoura Robe   (1916)
La gandoura verte
12⅞×9⅜″
Mr. and Mrs. Ralph F. Colin, New York

Studio, Quai St. Michel   (1916)
L'atelier, Quai Saint-Michel
57½×45¾″
The Phillips Collection, Washington, D.C.

49   The Painter and his Model   (1917)
Le peintre et son modèle
57⅞×38³/₁₆"
Musée National d'Art Moderne, Paris

43   The Green Robe   1916
Lorette sur fond noir
$28\frac{3}{4} \times 21\frac{1}{2}''$
Mr. and Mrs. Pierre Matisse

46   The Pewter Jug   (1916-17)
Le pot d'étain
36¼×25⅝″
The Baltimore Museum of Art, Cone Collection

The Pewter Jug   (1916-17)
Le pot d'étain
19¹¹/₁₆×15¾″   oil on wood
Professor Hans R. Hahnloser, Bern

40   Marguerite Matisse with Black Velvet Ribbon   (1916)
Marguerite Matisse au ruban noir de velours
7 ¼ × 6 ¾ ″
Private Collection, Paris

48   Marguerite in a Fur Hat   1917
Marguerite au chapeau de fourrure
16⅛×13″
Private Collection, Paris

50   Self Portrait   (1918)
Auto-portrait
$23\frac{5}{8} \times 21\frac{1}{4}''$
Jean Matisse, Paris

Woman with the Hat   (1920)
Femme au chapeau
23 × 19½″
Mr. and Mrs. Lee A. Ault, New York

53   Girl Reading   (1920)
Liseuse
$10^5/_8 \times 13^3/_4''$
Pierre Lévy, Troyes, France

White Plumes   (1919)
Les plumes blanches
$27\,^{9}/_{16} \times 23\,^{13}/_{16}''$
The Gothenburg Art Gallery, Sweden

52   The Artist and his Model   (1919)
L'artiste et son modèle
23 ½ × 28″
Dr. and Mrs. Harry Bakwin, New York

55   Interior at Nice   (1921)
Grand intérieur, Nice
52×35″
The Art Institute of Chicago, gift of Mrs. Gilbert W. Chapman

59   Checker Game and Piano Music   (1923)
Les joueurs de dames
29×36¼″
Private Collection, New York

The Moorish Screen   (1921-22)
Le paravent mauresque
36¼×29¼"
The Philadelphia Museum of Art, bequest of Lisa Norris Elkins

58   Odalisque in Red Trousers   (1922)
L'odalisque à la culotte rouge
26⁵/₁₆×33¹/₁₆″
Musée National d'Art Moderne, Paris

57   Nude with Green Shawl   (1921-
Nu au châle vert
35×45¾″
Lent anonymously

62   Still Life in the Studio   (1924)
Nature morte dans l'atelier
38½×31¼″
Mrs. Albert D. Lasker, New York

Nude Seated on a Blue Cushion   (1924)
Nu au coussin bleu
28½×23″
Mr. and Mrs. Sidney F. Brody, Los Angeles

67   Odalisque in an Armchair   1928
L'odalisque au fauteuil
$23\frac{5}{8} \times 28\frac{3}{4}''$
Musée d'Art Moderne de la Ville de Paris

60   Odalisque with Tambourine   (1923-24)
      Odalisque au tambourin
      36×25½″
      Lent anonymously

65   Lemons on a Pewter Plate   (1927)
Citrons sur plat d'étain
21 ½ × 25 ¾"
Mr. and Mrs. Nathan Cummings, Chicago

66   Decorative Figure on an Ornamental Background   (1927)
Figure décorative sur fond ornemental
$51^{3}/_{16} \times 38^{1}/_{2}''$
Musée National d'Art Moderne, Paris

64   Reclining Nude, Back   (1927)
Nu étendu de dos
26×36¼″
Private Collection, Paris

8   Girl in a Yellow Dress   (1929-31)
Jeune fille en jaune
$39\frac{3}{8} \times 32''$
The Baltimore Museum of Art, Cone Collection

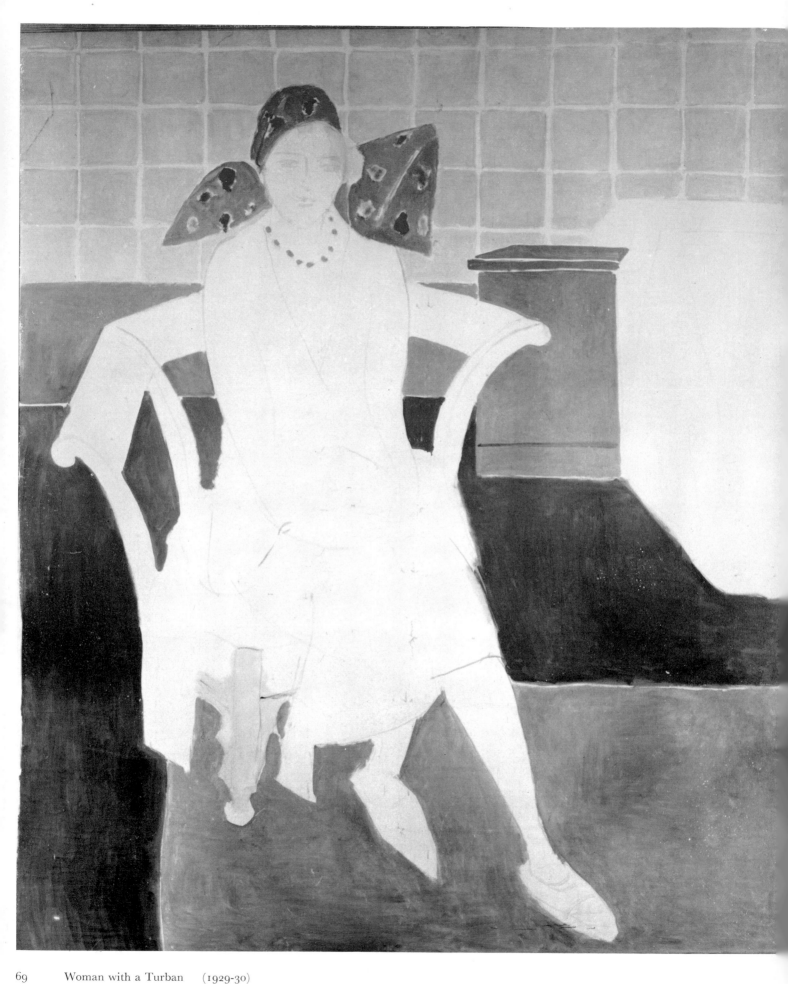

69   Woman with a Turban   (1929-30)
Femme au turban
70⅞×59⅞″
Private Collection, Paris

Pink Nude   1935
Nu rose
$26 \times 36 \frac{1}{2}''$
The Baltimore Museum of Art, Cone Collection

74 Nymph in the Forest (1936)
Nymphe dans la forêt
96×78″
Private Collection, Paris

Still Life with Three Vases   1935
Nature morte aux trois vases
28¾×23⅝″
Private Collection, Paris

70   Portrait of a Lady in White   (1933-34)
Portrait à la robe blanche
44 ½ × 28 ¾ "
Private Collection, Paris

The Dream   (1935)
Le rêve
31⅞×25⅝"
Mr. and Mrs. Pierre Matisse

75   Woman with Blue Jewel, Elena   1937
Femme au bijou bleu
21½ × 13¼″
Mr. and Mrs. Taft Schreiber, Beverly Hills

Odalisque with Striped Robe   1937
Odalisque, robe rayée, mauve et blanche
15 ×18″
Mr. and Mrs. Norton Simon, Los Angeles

77   Lady in Blue   1937
Grande robe bleue, fond noir
36½×29″
Mrs. John Wintersteen, President, The Philadelphia Museum of Art

The Conservatory   1938
Le jardin d'hiver
28¼×23½″
Mr. and Mrs. Joseph Pulitzer, Jr., St. Louis

78   Odalisque in a Red Coat   1937
Odalisque au manteau rouge et aux tulipes violettes
21 ¼ × 18″
Private Collection, New York

Pineapple and Anemones   1940
L'ananas et anémones
28½×35½"
Mrs. Albert D. Lasker, New York

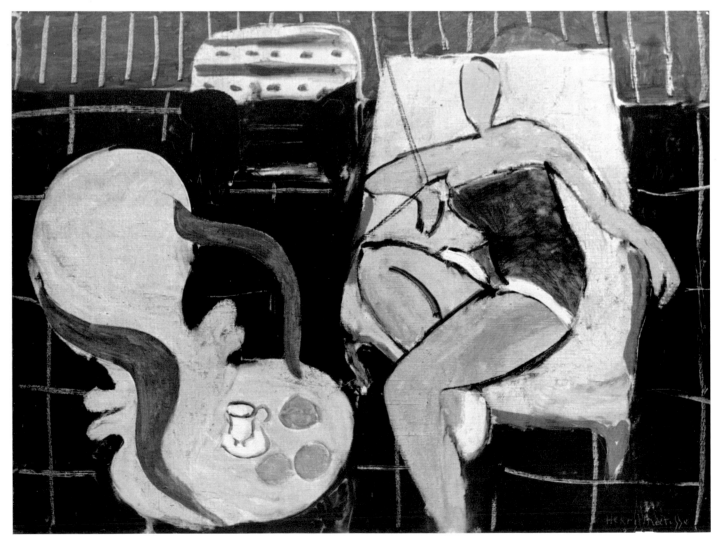

83   Dancer and Armchair, Black Background   (1942)
Danseuse, fond noir, fauteuil rocaille
19¾×25⅝″
Mrs. Marcel Duchamp, New York

Sleeping Woman 1940
La dormeuse
31⅞×25½″
Private Collection, Paris

82   The Black Door   1942
La porte noire
24 × 15″
Heinz Berggruen, Paris

86   Tabac Royal   1943
Intérieur à Nice
25 × 31 ½ "
Mrs. Albert D. Lasker, New York

85   The Lute   1943
        Le luth
        23³⁄₈×31³⁄₈″
        Mr. and Mrs. Sidney F. Brody, Los Angeles

Lemons and Saxifrages   1943
Citrons et saxifrages
21¼×31⅞″
Siegfried Rosengart, Lucerne

87   The Silence Living in Houses   1947
Le silence habité des maisons
21⅝ × 18⅛″
Private Collection, Paris

Interior with Figure   1947
Figure dans un intérieur
36¼ × 28¾″
Private Collection, Paris

89   The Pineapple   1948
L'ananas
45¾×35″
The Alex Hillman Corporation, New York

90   Large Interior in Red   1948
Grand intérieur rouge
57½ × 38¼"
Musée National d'Art Moderne, Paris

91   Interior with Black Fern   1948
Intérieur à la fougère noire
45⁹/₁₆×35″
Mr. and Mrs. Otto Preminger, New York

92   Woman in a Blue Gandoura Robe   1951
Portrait à la gandoura bleue
32 × 25 ½″
Jean Matisse, Paris

SCULPTURE

93a

93a   Profile of a Woman, Medaillon   1894
        Profil de Femme
        M 180 bis   Diameter 10″
        Private Collection, Paris

93   Jaguar Devouring a Hare—after Barye   (1899-1901)
        Jaguar dévorant un lièvre — d'après Barye
        M 144   9″
        Pierre Matisse

94   Old Woman, Bust   (1900)
        Buste ancien
        M 155   24½″
        The Joseph H. Hirshhorn Collection, New York

95   Study of a Foot   (1900)
        Etude de pied
        M 152   12″
        Charles E. Slatkin Galleries, New York

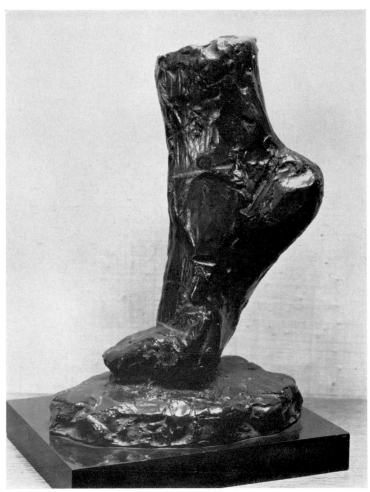

95

98

99

96   The Slave   (1900-03)
        Le serf
        M 121   36¼"
        The Joseph H. Hirshhorn Collection, New York

97   Madeleine I (round base)   (1901)
        M 123   23⅝"
        Charles E. Slatkin Galleries, New York

98   Madeleine II (square base)   (1903)
        M 153   23⅝"
        Private Collection, Paris

99   Woman Leaning on her Hands   (1905)
        Femme appuyée sur les mains
        M 124   5¼"
        Mr. and Mrs. Norton Simon, Los Angeles

100

101

100   Child's Head (Pierre)   (1905)
Tête d'enfant (Pierre)
M 138   6⅜″
Private Collection, New York

101   Head of a Faun   (1905)
Tête de faune
M 166   6¼″
Jean Matisse, Paris

102   Head of a Young Girl (Marguerite)   (1906)
Tête de fillette (Marguerite)
M 126   6½″
Frank Perls, Beverly Hills

103   Nude Braced, Arms on Head   (1906)
Nu campé, bras sur la tête
M 132   10″
Mrs. Bertram Smith, New York

104   Standing Nude   (1906)
Nu de fillette
M 139   19″
Private Collection, Paris

103

104

107

106

108

105

112

109

111

110

105	Reclining Figure in a Chemise (1906)	109	Reclining Nude I (1907)
	Nu couché à la chemise		*Nu couché I*
	M 127 6″		M 129 13⅞″
	The Joseph H. Hirshhorn Collection, New York		The Baltimore Museum of Art, Cone Collection
106	Small Head with Flat Nose (1906)	110	Decorative Figure (1908)
	Petite tête au nez camus		*Figure décorative*
	M 167 5½″		M 169 29″
	The Joseph H. Hirshhorn Collection, New York		The Joseph H. Hirshhorn Collection, New York
107	Small Head with Pompadour (1907)	111	Two Negresses (1908)
	Petite tête aux cheveux striés		*Deux négresses*
	M 170 4⅝″		M 122 18½″
	Jean Matisse, Paris		The Joseph H. Hirshhorn Collection, New York
108	Girl's Head with Necklace (1907)	112	Standing Torso, without Arms or Head (1909)
	Tête au collier		*Torse debout, sans bras ni tête*
	M 130 6⅛″		M 160 9¾″
	Mrs. Charles Payson, Manhasset, Long Island		The Joseph H. Hirshhorn Collection, New York

113

113

114

115

113 The Serpentine (1909)
    La serpentine
    M 142 22¼″
    Pierre Matisse

114 Seated Nude, Arm Behind Back (1909)
    Nu assis, bras derrière le dos
    M 131 11½″
    Private Collection, Paris

115 Seated Nude (Olga) (1910)
    Nu assis (Olga)
    M 143 16½″
    Jean Matisse, Paris

116

117

118

119

120

116   Head of Jeanette I   (1910-13)
Tête de Jeanette I
M 150   12½"
The Joseph H. Hirshhorn Collection, New York

117   Head of Jeanette II   (1910-13)
Tête de Jeanette II
M 149   10½"
The Joseph H. Hirshhorn Collection, New York

118   Head of Jeanette III   (1910-13)
Tête de Jeanette III
M 148   24"
Mr. and Mrs. Norton Simon, Los Angeles

119   Head of Jeanette IV   (1910-13)
Tête de Jeanette IV
M 151   24½"
The Joseph H. Hirshhorn Collection, New York

120   Head of Jeanette V   (1910-13)
Tête de Jeanette V
M 168   22⅞"
Jean Matisse, Paris

121   The Dance   (1911)
La danse
M 176   16⅛"
The Joseph H. Hirshhorn Collection, New York

122

123

124

125

122   Head of Marguerite   (1915)
Tête de Marguerite
M 125   12⅝″
Pierre Matisse

123   Crouching Nude, Arms Around the Right Leg   (1918)
Nu accroupi, bras autour de la jambe droite
M 157   9″
Paul Rosenberg and Co., New York

124   Crouching Venus   (1918)
Vénus accroupie
M 156   10¼″
Private Collection, New York

125   Large Seated Nude   (1922-25)
Grand nu assis
M 159   30¾″
The Minneapolis Institute of Arts

126   Small Nude in an Armchair   (1924)
Petit nu au canapé
M 184   9⅜″
Private Collection, New York

127

129

127   Henriette, Second State   (1927)
Henriette, deuxième état
M 140   12⅝
The San Francisco Museum of Art,
Harriet Lane Levy Bequest

128   Reclining Nude II   (1927-29)
Nu couché II
M 179   11″
Mr. and Mrs. Sidney F. Brody, Los Angeles

129   Henriette, Third State   (1929)
Tête souriante, Henriette, troisième état
M 163   15¾″
Private Collection, Paris

130   Reclining Nude III   (1929)
Nu couché III (torse rond)
M 154   7½″
Charles E. Slatkin Galleries, New York

128

130

131

133

132

131   Venus in a Shell   (1930)
Vénus à la coquille
M 173   12½″
Pierre Matisse

132   Tiari (with necklace)   (1930)
Le tiaré (au collier)
M 175   8⅛″
The Baltimore Museum of Art, Cone Collection

133   Venus in a Shell   (1932)
Vénus à la coquille
M 183   13½″
The Joseph H. Hirshhorn Collection, New York

134   Christ, Vence Chapel   (1950)
Christ, Chapelle de Vence
M 189   13¾″
Jean Matisse, Paris

134

135

136

135 Bas Relief I (1909)
   M 146 73¾×45⅝″
   Lent anonymously

136 Bas Relief II (1913)
   M 181 73⅝×45⅝″
   Lent anonymously

137 Bas Relief III (1916-17)
   M 145 73⅛×44⅞″
   Lent anonymously

138 Bas Relief IV (1930)
   M 147 73¼×44¾″
   Lent anonymously

  * Other casts of
   Bas Reliefs I, II, III, IV
   Installed in the sculpture garden
   of The Museum of
   Modern Art, New York

138

*

DRAWINGS

139

141

139   Seated Model, Hands Clasping Knee   (1900)
Figure assise
Pencil $13^1/_{16} \times 8^9/_{16}''$
The Metropolitan Museum of Art,
gift of Mrs. Florence Blumenthal   1910

141   Head of Marguerite Reading   (1905)
La liseuse (tête de Marguerite)
Pen and ink $15^5/_8 \times 20^1/_2''$
The Museum of Modern Art,
acquired through the Lillie P. Blies Bequest

142   Nude in a Chair   (1905)
Nu endormi dans une chaise
Brush with India ink $25^7/_8 \times 18^3/_8''$
The Art Institute of Chicago,
gift of Mrs. Potter Palmer

143   Nude with Pipes (Study for the *Joy of Life*)   (1906)
Etude pour la Joie de vivre
Pen and ink $18 \times 23^3/_4''$
Mr. and Mrs. Richard S. Davis, London

151   The Dance   (1909)
La danse
Pen and ink   6½×9″
Private Collection, Paris

152   The Dance   (1909)
La danse
11×9″
Private Collection, Paris

153   Seated Woman Clasping Her Right Knee   1909
Nu assis
Reed pen and ink   11⅝×9¼″
The Art Institute of Chicago,
gift of Emily Crane Chadbourne

154   Young Girl with Tulips   (1910)
Jeune fille aux tulipes
(Study for *Young Girl with Tulips*, Hermitage)
Private Collection, Paris

155   Study for Painting of Marguerite Matisse of 1910
Etude pour Jeune Fille au chat noir
(Marguerite Matisse)
Pencil   10¾×8¼″
The Art Institute of Chicago,
gift of Emily Crane Chadbourne

156   Jean and Pierre Matisse Playing Checkers   1911
Les joueurs de dames
Black crayon   19×24¾″
Private Collection, Paris

153

151

152

4

155

156

157

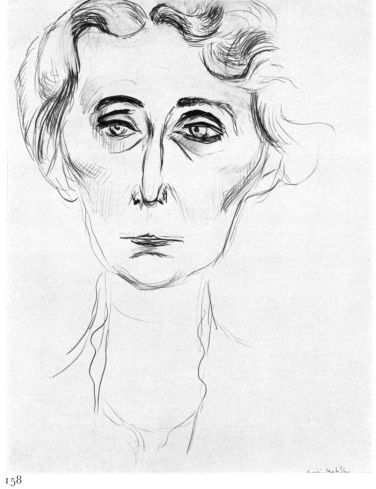

158

159

157   Portrait of Sergei I. Shchukin   (1912)
Portrait de Serge I. Stchoukine
Charcoal   19½×12″
Pierre Matisse

158   Portrait of Mrs. S. D. Warren,
née Mabel Bayard   (1913)
Pencil   11⅛×8½″
Museum of Fine Arts, Boston,
gift of Mrs. J. Gardner Bradley,
Mrs. Warren Thayer and Miss Sylvia Warren

159   Portrait of Miss Harriet Lane Levy   1913
Pencil   10⅞×8⅜″
The San Francisco Museum of Art,
Harriet Lane Levy Bequest

160   Elsa Glaser   1914
Pencil   11¼×9″
The Art Institute of Chicago,
gift of Mrs. Margaret Blake

161   Greta Prozor   (1916)
Charcoal   22½×15″
Private Collection, Paris

161

163   Antoinette Wearing Plumed Hat   (1919)
Antoinette au chapeau à plumes
Pen and ink   11 × 14″
The Art Institute of Chicago,
Gift of the Arts Club of Chicago

164   The Plumed Hat   1919
Le chapeau à plumes
Pencil   13¾ × 11½″
Mrs. Hildegard Ault Tjeder, New York

165   The Plumed Hat   1919
Le chapeau à plumes
Pencil   20⅞ × 14⅜″
The Detroit Institute of Arts,
bequest of John S. Newberry

164

163

165

166

168

169

174

171

166   Seated Nude with Arms Raised   (1920)
Nu assis aux bras levés
Charcoal   24 × 19½″
The Art Institute of Chicago, The Wirt D. Walker Fund

168   Nude with Raised Arms   (1923)
Nu aux bras levés
Charcoal   12⅜ × 18⅞″
Mr. and Mrs. James E. Pollak, Los Angeles

169   Standing Nude with Raised Arms   (1922-23)
Nu debout aux bras levés
Charcoal   20 × 15″
Heinz Berggruen, Paris

171   Nude, Back   (1927)
Nu de dos
(Study for *Reclining Nude, Back*, No. 64)
Pencil   11 × 14½″
Private Collection, Paris

172   Study for Decorative Figure   1927
Etude pour figure décorative
(Study for *Decorative figure
on an Ornamental Background*, No. 66)
Charcoal   24¾ × 19″
Private Collection, Paris

174   Standing Odalisque, Veiled   1930
Odalisque debout voilée
Crayon   12 × 9¼″
Frank Perls, Beverly Hills

176   Portrait of Dr. Claribel Cone   (1934)
Charcoal   23¼×16″
The Baltimore Museum of Art, Cone Collection

178   Nude in the Studio   1935
Nu dans l'atelier
Pen and ink   17¾×22⅜″
Private Collection, New York

179   Nude Seated on a Stool   1936
Nu au tabouret
Charcoal   20⅜×16″
Private Collection, Zurich

181   Self Portrait   1937
Auto-portrait
Charcoal   10⅛×10″
Private Collection, Paris

181

176

153

183

188

184

183   The Rumanian Blouse   (1937)
La blouse roumaine
Pen and black ink   25 × 19½″
The Baltimore Museum of Art, Cone Collection

184   Head of a Woman, I   1937
Tête de femme, I
Ink   24 × 16⅛″
Santa Barbara Museum of Art, gift of Wright Ludington

188   Two Women   1938
Deux figures de femmes
Pen and ink   15 × 20¼″
Private Collection, Paris

189   Seated Woman   1936
Femme assise
Charcoal   19¼ × 15″
Galerie Beyeler, Basel

192   Mother nursing Child   1939
Maternité
Charcoal   25½ × 19¾″
The Joseph H. Hirshhorn Collection

192

191

190   Sleeping Girl   1939
       La dormeuse
       (Study for *Sleeping Woman*, No 81)
       Pencil   21×16″
       Private Collection, Paris

191   Asiatic Lady   1939
       L'Asiatique
       Charcoal   23⅛×15¼″
       Dr. and Mrs. Franklin D. Murphy, Los Angeles

196   Theme A, Variation 5   1941
       Thèmes et variations, A 5
       Pen and ink   21⅛×16″
       Private Collection, Paris

197   Theme E, Variation 9   1941
       Thèmes et variations, E 9
       Pen and ink   21⅛×16″
       Private Collection, Paris

198   Theme F, Variation 1   1941
       Thèmes et variations, F 1
       Charcoal   15¾×20½″
       Grenoble, Musée de Peinture et de Sculpture

199   Theme F, Variations 3   1941
       Thèmes et variations, F 3
       Pen and ink, 20½×15¾″
       Grenoble, Musée de Peinture et de Sculpture

198

90

197

9

196

195

212

210

195   Theme A, Variation 2   1941
Thèmes et variations, A 2
Pen and ink   24¾×19⅝
P. N. Matisse Gallery, Beverly Hills

207   Branch of a Judas Tree   1942
Branche de l'arbre de Judas
Charcoal   10×15½"
Mr. and Mrs. John Rewald, New York

210   *Haiti*   (1943)
Ink   20½×15½"
Mr. and Mrs. Ray Stark, Los Angeles

212   Table, Still Life   1944
Nature morte sur une table
Pen and ink   15½×20½"
Dr. and Mrs. David I. Elterman,
Sherman Oaks, California

217   Interior   1948
Intérieur
Chinese ink   35×23"
Private Collection, Paris

217

216

216 Dahlias and Pomegranates   1947
Dahlias et grenades
Brush and ink   30⅛ × 22¼ ″
The Museum of Modern Art, New York,
Abby Aldrich Rockefeller Fund

219 Study for Christ Before Pilate,
Way of the Cross   (1949)
Etude pour Le Christ devant Pilate, Chemin de Croix
Chinese ink with brush   26 × 20 ″
Musée Matisse, Cimiez - Nice

220 Large Head of a Woman   (1952)
Grande tête de femme
Chinese ink   25⅞ × 19⅞ ″
Mrs. Vicci Sperry, Los Angeles

220

GRAPHICS

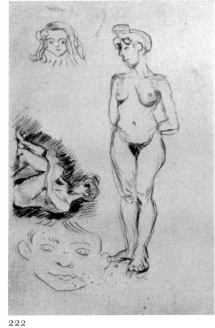

222

225

228

234

223
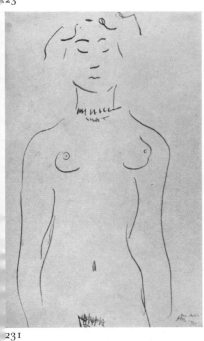

224

231

232

236

222
Sketches: Nudes and Children's Heads,
Jean and Marguerite (Second State)
(1900-01)
*Esquisses: nus et têtes d'enfants,
Jean et Marguerite (deuxième état)*
Drypoint Pl. 55 $5^{13}/_{16} \times 4''$
Jean Matisse, Paris

223
Studies of a Woman in Street Costume
(1900-01)
Deux études d'une femme en costume
Drypoint Pl. 56 $5\frac{1}{4} \times 3\frac{1}{2}''$
Jean Matisse, Paris

224
Three Studies of a Nude   (1900-01)
Nu, trois études
Drypoint Pl. 57 $5 \times 3\frac{1}{2}''$
The Art Institute of Chicago,
gift of Mr. and Mrs. Carl Schniewind

225
Self Portrait as an Etcher   (1903)
Le graveur, auto-portrait
Etching with drypoint Pl. 52 $5\frac{7}{8} \times 7\frac{7}{8}''$
The Metropolitan Museum of Art,
New York, Dick Fund

228
Nude   (1906)
Nu
Lithograph Pl. 29 $11^{3}/_{16} \times 9^{15}/_{16}''$
Jean Matisse, Paris

231
Standing Nude with Downcast Eyes   (1906)
Idole
Lithograph Pl. 2 bis $17\frac{1}{2} \times 8\frac{1}{2}''$
The Art Institute of Chicago,
The Alfred Stieglitz Collection

232   Upturned Head   (1906)
Tête renversée
Lithograph Pl. 5 $11\frac{1}{8} \times 10\frac{3}{4}''$
The Museum of Modern Art, New York,
gift of Abby Aldrich Rockefeller

234
Nude, The Large Woodcut   (1906)
Nu, le grand bois
Woodcut $18\frac{3}{4} \times 15''$
The Museum of Modern Art, New York,
gift of Mr. and Mrs. R. Kirk Askew, Jr.

235
Woodblock for: Nude, The Large Woodcut
(1906)
Bois pour: Nu, le grand bois
Woodblock $19\frac{1}{2} \times 15\frac{3}{4}''$
Frank Perls, Beverly Hills

236
Nude, The Light Woodcut   (1906)
Nu, le bois clair
Woodcut $13\frac{1}{4} \times 10''$

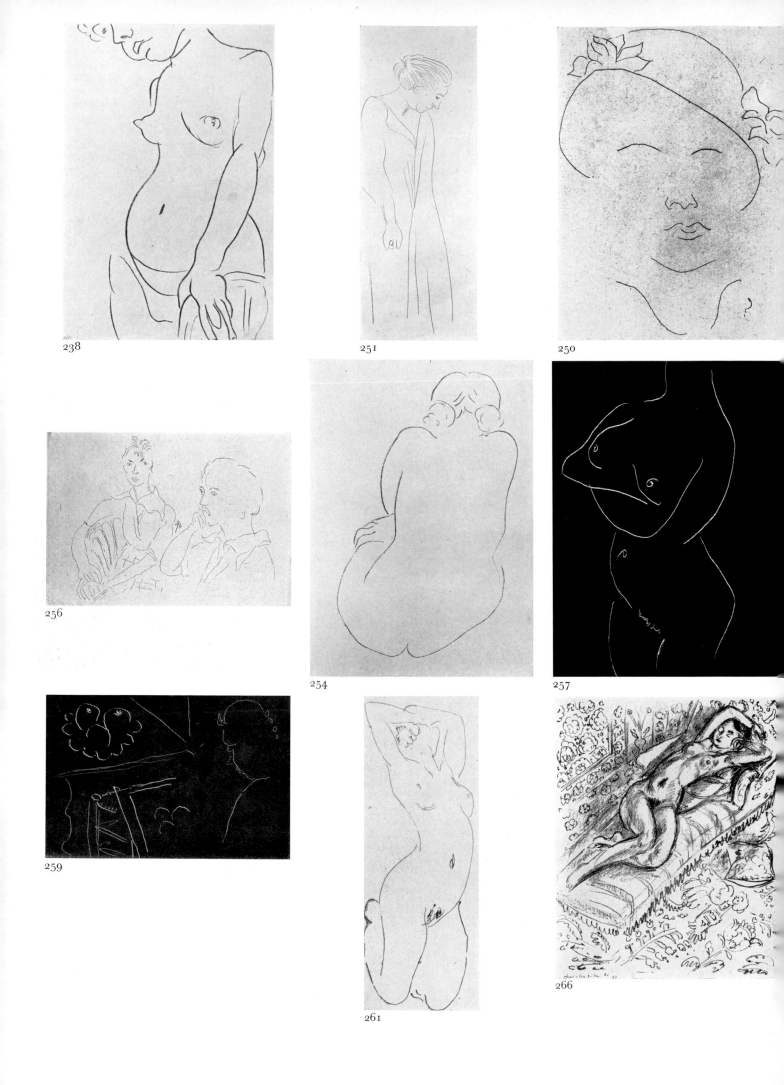

238

251

250

256

254

257

259

261

266

239

7

238
Torso, Face Partly Showing;
Nude with Face Half Hidden   (1912)
Torse au visage coupé
Lithograph Pl. 15   19¾×12″
The Art Institute of Chicago,
The Alfred Stieglitz Collection

239
Woman in Kimono (Mme Matisse)   (1914)
Femme en kimono (Mme Matisse)
Drypoint Pl. 12   6⁵/₁₆×2⅜″
The Brooklyn Museum,
gift of Louis E. Stern Foundation

250
Loulou in a Flowered Hat   (1914)
Loulou au chapeau à fleurs
Etching Pl. 41   7¹/₁₆×5″
The Museum of Modern Art, New York

251
Margot in a Japanese Robe   (1914)
Margot en robe japonaise
Etching Pl. 43   7¹¹/₁₆×4¼″
The Museum of Modern Art, New York

254
Seated Nude, Back Turned   (1914)
Nu assis, vue de dos
Lithograph Pl. 19   16⁹/₁₆×10⅜″
The Metropolitan Museum of Art,
New York, Rogers Fund

256
Double Portrait of Josette Gris   (1915)
Etching Pl. 32   5¹/₁₆×7⅛″
The Metropolitan Museum of Art,
New York, Dick Fund

257
Torso   (1916-17)
Torse
Monotype Pl. 13   6¹⁵/₁₆×5¹/₁₆″
The Museum of Modern Art, New York

275

258
Seated Nude with Arms Crossed   (1916-17)
Nu assis, bras croisés
Monotype   7×5¹/₁₆″
The Metropolitan Museum of Art,
New York, gift of Stephen Bourgeois

259
Interior, Artist Drawing Three Apples
(1916-17)
Intérieur, l'artiste dessine des pommes
Monotype   3¹³/₁₆×5⅞″
The Museum of Modern Art, New York,
gift of Abby Aldrich Rockefeller

261
Kneeling Nude   (1918)
Nu accroupi
Etching Pl. 104   6⅛×2⅛″
Jean Matisse, Paris

266
Reclining Nude on a Chaise Lounge   (1922)
Nu au canapé
Lithograph Pl. 35   19⅜×15¾″
University of California, Los Angeles,
Grunwald Graphic Arts Foundation

267
Female Nude   (1922)
Jeune fille nue
Lithograph Pl. 37   15×9½″
University of California,
Los Angeles, Norton Simon Collection

275
Girl with a Vase of Flowers   (1923)
Jeune fille au vase de fleurs
Lithograph Pl. 51   10⅞×7½″
Mr. and Mrs. Sidney F. Brody, Los Angeles

269
Odalisque with Magnolias   (1923)
Odalisque aux magnolias
Lithograph Pl. 42   *Essai*   11¼ × 15¾″
University of California, Los Angeles
Norton Simon Collection

277
Seated Nude with Arms Raised (1924)
Nu assis aux bras levés
Lithograph Pl. 55   24¼ × 18¹³/₁₆″
Mr. and Mrs. Sidney F. Brody, Los Angeles

281
Odalisque in Striped Pantaloons   (1925)
La culotte bayadère
Lithograph Pl. 64   21¼ × 17¼″
University of California,
Los Angeles, Norton Simon Collection

285
Seated Nude, Left Knee Raised   (1925)
Nu assis, jambe gauche levée
Lithograph Pl. 75   19½ × 16½″
University of California,
Los Angeles, Norton Simon Collection

288
Portrait of Cortot   (1926)
Drypoint Pl. 106   5³/₈ × 3⁵/₁₆″
University of California, Los Angeles,
Grunwald Graphic Arts Foundation

289
Alfred Cortot   (1926)
Lithograph Pl. 82   15 × 11½″
University of California,
Los Angeles, Norton Simon Collection

292
Two Odalisques   (1928)
Deux odalisques
Lithograph Pl. 109   18 × 30″
University of California, Los Angeles,
Grunwald Graphic Arts Foundation

294
Seated Nude, Left Knee Drawn to Chest
(1929)
*Femme nue serrant son genou gauche
contre sa poitrine*
Drypoint Pl. 116   5¹³/₁₆ × 4″
University of California, Los Angeles,
Grunwald Graphic Arts Foundation

296
Seated Woman, Arms on Knees   (1929)
Figure assise, bras sur les genoux
Etching Pl. 97   7⅞ × 5⅞″
University of California, Los Angeles,
Norton Simon Collection

308
Seated Girl with Bowl of Fish   (1929)
Nu assis, bocal de poissons
Etching Pl. 179   5⅞ × 8¾″
Mr. and Mrs. Sidney F. Brody, Los Angeles

269

277

288

289

294

308

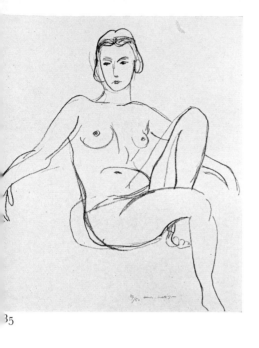

35

2

96

281

299

303

313

318

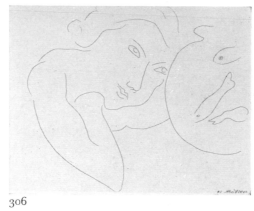

306

20

319

325

293
Reclining Nude with Louis XV Table
(1929)
Nu renversé, table Louis XV
Lithograph Pl. 118   22×18″
University of California,
Los Angeles, Norton Simon Collection

299
Woman Seated, Hands on Back of Chair
(1929)
Figure assise, mains sur le dos du fauteuil
Etching Pl. 126   6×4¾″
University of California,
Los Angeles, Norton Simon Collection

303
Woman, Full Face, Beside an Aquarium
(1929)
Femme de face, près d'un aquarium
Etching Pl. 142   3⅜×5″
Jean Matisse, Paris

306
Head of a Woman with Bowl of Fish
(1929)
Tête penchée, bocal de poissons
Etching Pl. 150   5¾×7½″
University of California,
Los Angeles, Norton Simon Collection

313
Persian Girl   (1929)
La Persane
Lithograph Pl. 100   17×11″
University of California,
Los Angeles, Norton Simon Collection

318
Self Portrait   (1936)
Auto-portrait
Lithograph   13×10″
The Art Institute of Chicago

319
Siesta   (1937)
La sieste
Linoleum cut Pl. 247   10¼×12″
University of California,
Los Angeles, Norton Simon Collection

320
The Beautiful Tahitian   (1937)
La belle Tahitienne
Linoleum cut Pl. 255   11×7¾″
University of California,
Los Angeles, Norton Simon Collection

325
Head (Full Face)   (1948)
Tête de face
Aquatint Pl. 342   12⅜×9⅞″
The Museum of Modern Art,
New York, Curt Valentin Bequest

326
Head (Profile)   (1948)
Aquatint Pl. 359   16¹⁵/₁₆×13¾″
The Museum of Modern Art,
New York, Curt Valentin Bequest

GOUACHES DÉCOUPÉES

342

343

335   Still Life   (1941)
Nature morte
23 5/8 × 32″
Pierre Matisse

342   Seated Blue Nude III   1952
Nu bleu III
45 3/4 × 32″   Signed and dated lower center
Jean Matisse, Paris

343   Seated Blue Nude IV   1952
Nu bleu IV
40 1/2 × 30 1/4″   Signed and dated lower center
Jean Matisse, Paris

345   The Sheaf (design for wall ceramic)   1953
La gerbe
115 3/4 × 137 3/4″
UCLA Art Galleries, Los Angeles

345

SELECTED BIBLIOGRAPHY

This bibliography begins in 1951, the date of the publication of Matisse, His Art and His Public, *by Alfred H. Barr, Jr., (New York, The Museum of Modern Art).*
In the preparation of this exhibition the debt to Dr. Barr's authoritative book was paramount and the reader is referred to it for bibliographical information prior to 1951.

Monographs

BARR, Alfred H., Jr. *Matisse: His Art and His Public.* New York: The Museum of Modern Art, 1951. 591 p., ill., plates.

CASSOU, Jean. *Henri Matisse, Carnet de Dessins.* Paris: Huguette Berès, Berggruen & Cie, 1955. Vol. I, 27 p. text; Vol. II, 44 drawing plates.

DIEHL, Gaston. *Henri Matisse.* Paris: Fernand Nathan, 1952. 48 p., plates.

DIEHL, Gaston. *Henri Matisse.* Paris: Pierre Tisné, 1954. 167 p., 140 plates, part. color. Notices by Agnès Humbert. *Note bibliographique,* p. 157-158.

DUTHUIT, Georges. *Matisse: Période fauve.* Paris: Fernand Hazan, 1956. 16 p., plates. Petite encyclopédie de l'Art, 2. English edition: *Matisse, Fauve Period* (New York: Tudor, 1956).

ESCHOLIER, Raymond. *Matisse, Ce Vivant.* Paris: Arthème Fayard, 1956. 286 p., ill., part color. English edition: Matisse from the Life (London: Faber and Faber, 1960). Introduction and notes by R. H. Wilenski. Translated from the French by Geraldine and H.M. Colvile.

FERRIER, Jean-Louis. *Matisse 1911-1930.* Paris: Fernand Hazan, 1961. Text in French. 27 p., 16 color plates.

GEORGE, Waldemar. *Matisse.* Arcueil: Laboratoire Chanterneau, 1955. 16 p., ill.

GREENBERG, Clement. *Henri Matisse.* New York: Harry N. Abrams, in association with Pocket Books, c. 1953. 80 p., 39 plates.

HILDEBRANDT, Hans. *Henri Matisse: Frauen, 32 Radierungen.* Leipzig: Insel-Verlag, 1953. 13 p., plates.

HUMBERT, Agnès. *Henri Matisse: Dessins.* Paris: Fernand Hazan, 1956. 12 p., plates. Bibliothèque Aldine des Arts, 37.

HUNTER, Sam. *Henri Matisse, 1869-1954.* New Yo: Book-of-the-Month Club, 1956. 31 p., 24 color pla Metropolitan Museum of Art Miniatures.

JEDLICKA, Gotthard. *Die Matisse Kapelle in Ver: Rosenkranz Kapelle der Dominikanerinnen.* Frankfurt: Su kamp, c. 1955. 95 p., plates.

KAMPIS, Antal. *Matisse.* Budapest: Képzömuvész: alap Kiadóvàllalata, 1959. 32 p., plates.

LASSAIGNE, Jacques. *Matisse.* Geneva: Skira, 19 138 p., plates, part color. Translated by Stuart Gilb Selected bibliography, p. 125-128. The Taste of Time, no. 30.

LIEBERMAN, William S. *Etchings by Matisse.* New Yo The Museum of Modern Art, 1955. 24 plates. Distribu by Simon and Schuster.

LIEBERMAN, William S. *Matisse: 50 Years of His Gra Art.* New York: George Braziller, 1956. 150 p., ill. plat

PACH, Walter. *Henri Matisse, a Gallery of Wom A Portfolio of Sketches.* New York: Beechhurst Press, c. 19 44 p., ill., plates.

REVERDY, Pierre and DUTHUIT, Georges. *The Works of Henri Matisse, 1950-1954.* New York: Harco Brace, 1958. 183 p., plates, 40 color. Matisse compc cover especially for this volume, which is no. 35-3€ Verve, French edition.

SELZ, Jean. *Matisse.* New York: Crown, 1964. Tr. lated from French by A.P.H. Hamilton. 94 p., 53 c plates.

VERDET, André. *Prestiges de Matisse, précédé de à Matisse, entretiens avec Matisse.* Paris: Emile-Paul, 1 126 p., ill., plates.

General References

ACEVEDO, C. de. *Dibutade; ou, La représentation picturale des formes.* Paris: Arthème Fayard, 1951. 150 p., plates. Preface by A. Maurois.

Art and Education. A collection of essays. 3d ed. Merion, Pa. Barnes Foundation Press, 1954. 316 p. 1st ed., 1929. 2d ed., 1947. Comparative Studies of Renoir, Cézanne, Matisse, Stravinsky.

BARR, Alfred H., Jr. *Masters of Modern Art.* New York: The Museum of Modern Art, 1954. pgs 47, 55, 227, 228; pls. 41, 90.

BARRY, Joseph A. *Left Bank, Right Bank: Paris and Parisians.* New York: W.W. Norton, c. 1951. 267 p.

BAYÓN, Damián Carlos. *Principales corrientes y artistas en la pintura del siglo XX.* Caracas: Sociedad de Amigos del Museo de Bellas Artes, 1958. 73 p., ill. Text edited by Eva B. Bustamente.

BROCKWAY, Wallace. *Renoir to Matisse: The Albert D. Lasker Collection.* New York: Simon and Schuster, 1957. pgs 103, 105, 107, 109, 111, 113, 115, 117, 119; all color plates with notes. Introduction by Alfred Frankfurter.

CARRIERI, Raffaele. *Pittori di ieri e di oggi.* Milan: Ferrania, 1953. 119 p., plates. Edizione della rivista Ferrania, no. 3.

CARTIER-BRESSON, Henri. *The Decisive Moment.* New York: Simon and Schuster, 1952. 52 p.; Cover designed and executed by Henri Matisse. French edition: Paris, Verve.

CHARBONNIER, Georges. *Le monologue du peintre.* Vol Paris: René Julliard, 1960. 211 p., ill.

CLAPARÈDE, Jean. *Dessins des XIXe et XXe Siè (Museé Fabre, Montpellier.) Editions des Musées N: naux, Palais du Louvre. Pls. 167-173. Series: Invent des collections publiques françaises, Vol. 6.

COUTURIER, M.A., O.P.; M.R. CAPELLADES, A COCGNAC and L.B. RAYSSIGIUER. *Les Chapelles du saire à Vence par Matisse et de Notre-Dame-du-Haut à Ronc par Le Corbusier.* Paris: Les Editions du Cerf. 1955. 10 plates.

DAVID, Christoph W., ed. *Moderne Kirchen: Ma Vence; Fernand Léger, Audincourt; Le Corbusier, Ronch Zurich: Die Arche, 1957. 80 p., plates. Edited in c oration with Raymond Escholier.

ESCHOLIER, Raymond. *Prisme des Arts.* Paris: P rama de l'Art Présent, 1957. "D'où vient Matiss 5 p., ill.

FLANNER, Janet. *Men and Monuments.* New Y Harper, 1957. 297 p. "King of the Wild Beasts", p. 71-

FOWLIE, Wallace. *... Mallarmé.* Chicago: Unive of Chicago Press, c. 1953. 299 p., plates. Includes 1c drawings by Matisse.

GIEURE, Maurice. *Initiation à l'œuvre de Picasso.* F Editions des deux Mondes, 1951. "Constantes esthét de Cézanne, Picasso, Matisse et Braque", p. 312

GUERRISI, Michele. *L'errore di Cézanne*. Pisa: Nistri-Lischi, 1954. "L'arabesco di Matisse", p. 143-173.

HERON, Patrick. *The Changing Forms of Art*. London: Routledge and Kegan Paul, 1955. "Henri Matisse", p. 144-146, 232-233.

JOLLOS, Waldemar. *Arte Tedesca fra le due Guerre*. Verona: Mondadori, 1955. 250 p., plates. Introduction by Luigi Rognoni. Biblioteca contemporanea Mondadori.

KIDD, Steven R. *The Abby Aldrich Rockefeller Memorial Window*. Pocantico Hills: Union Church, 1956. 15 p., ill. (On Matisse's window design, p. 15.)

KOHN, Heinz. *Neuere Meister aus dem Museum Folkwang zu Essen*, Cologne: E.A. Seeman, c. 1952. 14 p., plates.

KUENY, Gabrielle and Germain Viatte. *Dessins Modernes*. (Grenoble, Musée de Peinture et de Sculpture.) Paris: Editions des Musées Nationaux, Palais du Louvre, 1963. Pls. 129-155. Series: Inventaires des collections publiques françaises, Vol. 8.

LANGUI, Emile. *50 Years of Modern Art*. New York: Praeger, 1959. pgs 10, 105-110, 317. German edition: Cologne: Schanberg, 1959.

LIBERMAN, Alexander. *The Artist in His Studio*. New York: Viking Press, 1960. Foreword by James Thrall Soby. 21-24; pls. 22-30. Canadian edition: Toronto: Macmillan Co. of Canada, 1960.

MAN, Felix H., ed. *Eight European Artists*. London: William Heinemann, 1954. 24 p., plates. Includes writings by each artist, facsimiles of their handwriting, views of studios, and biographical notes.

MAYWALD, Wilhelm. *Portrait-Atelier*. Zurich: Die Arche, 1958. 144 p., plates. Includes photographs of Artists, statements by artists, and facsimiles of the artists' signatures.

MOURLOT, Fernand. *Art in Posters: Complete Original Posters of Braque, Chagall, Dufy, Léger, Matisse, Miro, Picasso*. Montecarlo: André Sauret. New York: George Braziller, 1959.

MÜNSTERBERG, Hugo. *Twentieth Century Painting*. New York: Philosophical Library, 1951. 102 p., plates.

MYERS, Bernard. *The Development of Modern Art*. Series of articles extracted from *American Artists*, 15, no. 7 (Dec. 1951); 16, no. 6, (June 1952). "Matisse and the Fauves", p. 70-72, 85.

MYERS, Bernard. *Fifty Great Artists*. New York: Bantam Books, c. 1953. 238 p., plates.

POLLACK, Barbara. *The Collectors: Dr. Claribel and Miss Etta Cone*. Indianapolis: Bobbs-Merrill, 1962. 320 p., ill. With excerpts by Gertrude Stein.

READ, Herbert. *The Art of Sculpture*. New York: Pantheon, 1956. The A.W. Mellon Lectures in the Fine Arts for 1954, National Gallery of Art, Washington, D.C. Bollinger Series, No. XXXV-3. pgs 93, 109.

READ, Herbert. *A Concise History of Modern Sculpture*. New York: Praeger, 1964. pgs 28, 30-42, 34, 41, 51, 140, 156, 250; pls. 24-39.

RITCHIE, Andrew Carnduff. *Sculpture of the 20th Century*. New York: The Museum of Modern Art, 1952. pgs 58, 59, 117, 132-133.

SCHMIDT, Georg. *Petite histoire de la peinture moderne de Daumier à Chagall*. Neuchâtel: Griffon, 1956. 112 p., plates.

SHACK, William. *Art and Argyrol: The Life and Career of Dr. Albert C. Barnes*. New York and London: Thomas Yoseloff, 1960. "Pertaining to Matisse, Mostly", p. 223-238.

SIMA, Michel. *21 Visages d'Artistes*. Paris: Fernand Nathan, 1959. Preface by Jean Cocteau; writings in facsimile by each artist. 159 p., plates. p. 17-18, pls. 93-99. Translation from French by Gloria Levy: New York, Tudor, 1959.

SOBY, James Thrall. *Modern Art and the New Past*. Norman: University of Oklahoma Press, 1957. Introduction by Paul J. Sachs. Collection of articles originally published in *Saturday Review*. "Matisse Reconsidered", p. 87-92.

UNTERMEYER, Louis. *Makers of the Modern World*. New York: Simon and Schuster, 1955. 809 p.

Writings by Matisse

Jazz, Munich, R. Piper & Co., 1957, 51 pgs; for The Museum of Modern Art, New York. 17 of the 20 color plates have been reproduced from the 1947 Paris publication of Editions Verve. English translation by Monroe Wheeler.

Portraits, Monte Carlo, Editions André Sauret, 1954, 17 pgs., 93 plates of which 33 are in color; the frontispiece is an original lithograph. The work was composed by Henri Matisse who also did the cover especially for the volume. Edition of 2,850 numbered copies of which 500 were in English.

Art News and Review (London), Feb. 6, 1956, "Looking at Life with the Eyes of a Child", by H. Matisse.

Farbe und Gleichnis. Gesammelte Schriften, by Henri Matisse, Zurich, Arche Verlag, 1955. Writings by Matisse with souvenirs by Hans Purrmann.

XXe Siècle, N.S., No. 2, January 1952, pgs. 66-67, "Témoignages: Henri Matisse". (Propos recueillis par Maria Luz et approuvés par Henri Matisse).

Miscellaneous Articles

ALAZARD, Jean. "Deux Peintres: Henri Matisse", *Revue Méditerranée*, 15 (1955), 405-409.

BALLOU, M.G. ",Interior with Etruscan Vase' by Matisse", *Cleveland Museum Bulletin*, 39 (Dec. 1952), 239-240.

BAZAINE, Jean. "Clarté de Matisse", *Derrière le Miroir* no. 46-47 (May 1952).

BELL, Clive. "Henri Matisse", *Apollo*, 60 (Dec. 1954), 151-156.

BERNIER, R. "Le Musée Matisse à Nice", *L'Oeil*, no. 105 (Sept. 1963), 20-29.

BOWNESS, A. "Four Drawings by Modigliani and Matisse", *Connoisseur* 150 (June 1962), 116-120.

BREESKIN, A.D. "Matisse and Picasso as Book Illustrators", *Baltimore Museum News*, 14 (May 1951), 1-3.

BREESKIN, A.D. "Accolade to Henri Matisse", *Baltimore Museum News*, 15 (May 1952), 1-4.

CASSOU, Jean. "Henri Matisse, coin d'atelier", *Quadrum*, no. 5 (1958), 68-69. (English summary, p. 90.)

"Chapelle de Vence", *L'Art sacré*, no. 11-12 (July-Aug. 1951). 32 pp., ill.

"Chapel of the Rosary, Vence", *Magazine of Art*, 44 (Nov. 1951), 271-272.

CHASTEL, André. "Le visible et l'occulte, Matisse et Klee", *Médecine de France*, no. 61 (1955), 41-42.

COCTEAU, Jean. "Matisse et Picasso", *Habitat*, no. 73 (Sept. 1963), 58-60.

COGNIAT, Raymond. "Henri Matisse", *Goya*, Madrid, II (1955-56), 28-33.

COMTESSE, Alfred. "Le troisième grand livre d'Henri Matisse", *Stultifera Navis*, 7 (1955), 87-90.

COOPER, Douglas. "Matisse Museum", *New Statesman and Nation*, 65 (Feb. 1, 1963), 162.

COSTESCO, Eleonora. "Trois dessins de Matisse", *Art Rep. Pop. Roumaine*, 14 (1957), 67-70 (Two variants of "La blouse roumaine", Bucharest Museum).

"La Cote: Derain et Matisse", *L'Oeil*, no. 1 (Jan. 1955), 40-41.

COURTHION, Pierre. "Le papier collé du Cubisme à nos jours" and "Les papiers découpés d'Henri Matisse", *XXᵉ Siècle*, n.s., no. 6 (Jan. 1956), 3 60.

DANIEL-ROPS. "L'acte de foi de Matisse", *Jardin des Arts*, no. 17 (1956), 257-261.

DEGAND, Leon. "Pour une révision des valeurs; Matisse, un génie?" *Aujourd'hui et Architecture*, 2d year, 28-31. no. 10 (Nov. 1956),

"Dessins récents dans l'exposition à la Galerie Maeght", *Cahiers d'Art*, 27, no. 1 (1952), 55-66.

"Deux faux tableaux de Matisse", *Cahiers d Art*, 27, no. 1 (1952), 94.

"Deux grandes rétrospectives à Paris: Fernand Léger et Henri Matisse", *XXᵉ Siècle*, n.s., no. 8 (Jan. 1957) 77.

DORIVAL, Bernard. "Fauves: The Wild Beasts Tamed", *Arts News Annual*, 22 (1952), 98-129.

DORIVAL, Bernard. "Matisse", *Bull. Soc. Amis Musée de Dijon* (1958-1960), 69-73.

DUTHUIT, Georges. "Material and Spiritual Worlds of Henri Matisse", trans. Louise Varèse, *Art News*, 55 (Oct. 1956), 22-25.

DUTHUIT, Georges, "Matisse and Courbet", *Ark*, no. 14 (1955), 12-13. (Interview with M. Georges Duthuit on the occasion of his visit to the Royal College of Art, March 1955.)

ELLIOT, Eugene Clinton. "Some Recent Conceptions of Color Theory", *Journal of Aesthetics*, 18 (June 1960), 494-503. (Study of the use of color by Matisse, Gris, Kandinsky, Hiler, and Hofmann.)

ESCHOLIER, Raymond. "Matisse et le Maroc", *Jardin des Arts*, no. 24 (1956), 705-712.

"February 23, 1957—Opening of the Cone Wing: Matisse Paintings and Drawings", *Baltimore Museum News*, 20 (Feb. 1957), 1-3, 6-7, 12-13.

FLANNER, Janet. "King of the Wild Beasts", *New Yorker*, 27 (Dec. 22, 1951), 30-32; (Dec. 29, 1951), 26-28.

GASSER, Manuel. "Exhibition Posters by Famous Artists", *Graphis*, 16 (March 1960), 108-119. (Reproductions 9, 14, 18, 19, 27, with English, German, and French texts.)

GELDZAHLER, Henry. "Two Early Matisse Drawings", *Gazette des Beaux-Arts*, ser. 6, vol. 60 (Nov. 1962), 497-505. (French summary; bibliography.)

GOTTLIEB, Carla. "The Joy of Life: Matisse, Pica and Cézanne", *College Art Journal*, 18 (Winter 195 106-116.

GOTTLIEB, Carla. "Role of the Window in the of Matisse", *Journal of Aesthetics*, 22, no. 4 (Summer 196 393-423. (Bibliography.)

HAMMARÉN, Carl-Erik. "Kapellet i Vence", *Palet* 17th year, no. 2 (1956), 42.

HASEGAWA, S. "Matisse through Japanese Eye *Art News*, 53 (April 1954), 27-29, 65, 66.

"Henri Matisse", *Baltimore Museum News*, 18 (I 1954), 6-7.

"Henri Matisse: A small Chapel in France and a M numental Art Exhibition at The Museum of Mod Art (N.Y.)", *Life*, 31 (Nov. 26, 1951), 108-116.

HOCTIN, Luce. "Renaissance of Church Art in Franc *Graphis*, 13 (May 1957), 224-235.(Chapel at Ver 226-229.)

HOLM, Arne E. "Matisse's Kapell i Vence", *Ku Idag* (Oslo), 20. hft., no. 4 (1951), 32-51. (Includes Eng translation.)

HOLM, Arne E. "Henri Matisse som Skulptø *Kunsten Idag* (Oslo), 33, no. 3 (1955), 26-45.

"Homage to Matisse", *Yale Literary Magazine* (Fall 19 Includes writings by Alfred H. Barr, Jr., Marcel Ducha George Heard Hamilton, George Kirgo, Jacques I chitz, Leonid Massine, Darius Milhaud, Henri Pe Alice B. Toklas, and Frank Anderson Trapp.

HÜTTINGER, Eduard. "Henri Matisse Sculto *Arte Figur. Ant. Mod.*, no. 4 (1959), 40-44.

HUMBERT, Agnès. "Les Fauves et le Fauvisn *Jardin des Arts*, no. 12 (1955), 713-720.

ITALIAANDER, Rolf. "Henri Matisse baut eine Kirc *Kunstwerk* (Baden-Baden), 5. Jahr, Hft. 1 (1951), 52 (Chapel at Vence.)

LANGLAND, J. "Henri Matisse" (poem), *Nation*, (April 30, 1955), 369.

LASSAIGNE, Jacques. "Les grandes gouaches décou de Matisse", *Lettres Françaises* (Aug. 6, 1959).

LEYMARIE, Jean. "Le Jardin de Paris", *Quad* Brussels, no. 7 (1959).

LEYMARIE, Jean. "Les grandes gouaches décou à la Kunsthalle de Berne", *Quadrum*, Brussels, n (1959), 103-114, 192. (English summary, p. 192.)

LIEBERMAN, William S. "Henri Matisse, 1869-19 *Print*, 10 (Aug. 1956), 17-28.

LIEBERMAN, William S. "Illustrations by F Matisse", *Magazine of Art*, 44 (Dec. 1951), 308 (Bibliography.)

"Matisse: A Rare Collection Record (Cone Cc tion)," *Vogue*, 125 (March 1955), 132-135.

"Matisse and His Masterpiece (Vence Chapel)", *A can Society of Legion of Honor Magazine*, 28 (1957), 2

"Ur Matisse Anteckningar", *Paletten*, 19th year, (1958), 40-44. (Draftsman.)

"Matisse Chapel", *Architectural Forum*, 96 (May 1 148-153.

"Die Matisse Kapelle in Vence", *Werk*, 40 (June 1 200-204.

"Matisse Scultore al Kunsthaus", *Emporium*, no (Oct. 1959), 176-177, 179.

"Matisse's Last Mural, Installed in California: Wall in the Brody Home, Los Angeles", *Art New* (June 1956), 30-31, 67.

MATTHAIS, Lisa. "De Portugisiska Breven", *Ord ock Bild* (1953), 147-255. (Illustrations of the portraits of the *Religieuse Portugaise* by Henri Matisse and Amedeo Modigliani.)

"Minneapolis Institute Purchase: Boy with Butterfly Net", *Minneapolis Institute Bulletin*, 42 (Feb. 7, 1953), 26-29.

"Modern Art and Modern Taste: The Albert D. Lasker Collection", *Art News Annual*, 27 (1958), 35-36.

MORLEY, Grace L. McCann. "The Matisse Exhibition" and "Works by Henri Matisse in the San Francisco Region", *San Francisco Museum Quarterly*, 2d ser., 1, no. 1-2 (1952) 13-20.

MULLALY, Terence. "The Fauves", *Apollo*, 64 (Dec. 1956), 184-186.

MURCIA, M. "Homage to Henri Matisse", *Marg*, 8, no. 3 (June 1955), 91-94.

MYERS, Bernard. "Matisse and the Fauves", *American Artist*, 15, no. 7 (Dec. 1951), 70-72.

NEWBERRY, J.S., Jr. "Matisse Drawing: ,Still Life with Fruit and Flowers'," *Detroit Institute Bulletin*, 31 no. 1 (1951-52), 21-23.

PERNOUD, Régine. "The Chapel of the Rosary", *San Francisco Museum Quarterly*, 2d ser., 1, no. 1-2 (1952), 13-20.

PITTALUGA, Mary. "Il Giudizio di Hans Purrmann sui Maestri Francesi", *Commentari*, 9 (1960), 284-296. (Judgments on Cézanne and Matisse.)

RAYMOND, Marie. Matisse contra de Abstracten", *Kroniek van Kunst en Kultur*, Amsterdam, 13de jaar, no. 10 (Dec. 1953), 227-229.

ROSENTHAL, G. "Matisse's Reclining Figures: A Theme and Its Variations", *Baltimore Museum News*, 19 (Feb. 1956), 10-15.

ROUVEYRE, A. "Matisse Evoqué", *Revue des Arts*, 6 (June 1956), 66-74.

SALLES, Georges. "Visit to Matisse", *Art News Annual*, 21 (1951), 37-39, 79-81.

SCHNIER, J. "Matisse from a Psychoanalytic Point of View", *College Art Journal*, 12, no. 2 (1953), 110-117. (Bibliography.)

SLIVKA, R. "Matisse Chasubles Designed for the Vence Chapel", *Craft Horizon*, 16 (Jan. 1956), 22-25.

SMITH, Elaine. "Matisse and Rouault Illustrate Baudelaire", *Baltimore Museum News*, 19 (Oct. 1955), 1-9.

SNODGRASS, W.D. "Matisse: The Red Studio", *Portfolio and Art News Annual*, no. 3 (1960), 90-91.

SOLMI, Sergio. "Disegni di Matisse", *Sele Arte*, Florence, 1, no. 2 (Sept.-Oct. 1952), 54-57.

SOWERS, R. "Matisse and Chagall as Craftsmen", *Craft Horizon*, 22 (Jan. 1962), 28-31.

"Statements on Matisse by Apollinaire, Berenson, Kandinsky, Picasso, Fernande Olivier and Léger", *Art*, London, 1 (Nov. 26, 1954), 8.

TÉRIADE, E. "Matisse Speaks", *Art News Annual*, 21 (1951), 40-77.

"Three Sculptures in the Cone Collection: 'Reclining Nude', 'Slave', 'Venus in a Shell'", *Baltimore Museum News*, 20 (Feb. 1957), 10-11.

"Vestments Designed by Matisse for the Vence Chapel", *Arts and Architecture*, 73 (May 1956), 35. Ill.

VIGNORELL, Don Valerio. "La Lezione di Vence", *Arte Cristiana* (1954), 33-38.

WIND, Edgar. "Traditional Religion and Modern Art", *Art News*, 52 (May 1953), 19-22. (Discussion including work of Matisse, especially Vence, in relation to Rouault of a religious artist.)

EXHIBITIONS AND CATALOGUES

1951-52 THE MUSEUM OF MODERN ART,
New York
" Henri Matisse " Gallery imprint, 32 p.
(Introduction by Alfred H. Barr Jr.)
November 13 – January 13
Also shown:
CLEVELAND MUSEUM OF ART,
February 5 – March 16

THE ART INSTITUTE OF CHICAGO
April 1 – May 4
SAN FRANCISCO MUSEUM OF ART
May 22 – July 6

GALERIE SAMLAREN, Stockholm
H. Matisse, Thèmes et Variations:
Le Rêve – La Chapelle
December – January

1952 MUSÉE DES ARTS DÉCORATIFS, Paris
"50 ans de Peinture Française
dans les collections particulières –
De Cézanne à Matisse"
March – April

MUNICIPAL DEPT. OF ART, Los Angeles
"Selection from The Museum
of Modern Art Retrospective"
July 21 – August 17
Also shown:
PORTLAND ART MUSEUM
September 12 – October 10

Inauguration of the MUSÉE MATISSE
at Le Cateau, Nord, in the presence
of Mme Georges Duthuit and Jean Matisse
Inaugurated by Georges Salles
November 9

STATE ART GALLERY, Raleigh, N. C.
"Matisse-Lithographs, Etchings, Bronzes"
February 10 – March 2

GALERIE MAEGHT, Paris
"Dessins Récents de Henri Matisse"
opened May 16

FRANK PERLS GALLERY, Beverly Hills
"Henri Matisse" (Loan exhibition from
Southern California Museums & Collectors)
Poster and Catalog
May 22 – June 30

BERGGRUEN & CIE., Paris
"Henri Matisse: Gravures à la gouge, aquatintes"
Gallery imprint, 24 p.
June 19 – July 12

1952 GRANDE SALLE DES EXPOSITIONS DE
LA RÉSERVE, Knokke-Le-Zoute
"Matisse"
Bruxelles: Editions de la Connaissance, S.A., 1952, 35
(Foreword by Georges Duthuit)
July 12 – August 31

GALERIE BLANCHE, Stockholm (cat.nr.49)
"Henri Matisse" – Gallery imprint, 3 p.
September – October

GALERIE DE BEAUNE, Paris
"Exposition d'Oeuvres de Matisse"
(At the time of the publication by Editions
Emile-Paul of *Prestiges de Matisse* by André Verdet)
December 12 – December 25

1952-53 GALERIE KLEBER, Paris
"Posters by Mourlot"
December 5 – January

1953 THE MUSEUM OF MODERN ART,
New York:" Les Fauves". Also shown in
Minneapolis, San Francisco, Toronto.
Foreword by John Rewald

THE TATE GALLERY, London
"Matisse – Sculpture, also 3 Paintings with Studies"
Gallery imprint, 8 p.
(Foreword by Philip James; Introduction by Jean Cass
January 9 – February 22

SOCIETY OF THE FOUR ARTS, Palm Beach
"The Art of Henri Matisse"
Gallery imprint, 16 p.
February 6 – March 1

CURT VALENTIN GALLERY, New York
"The Sculpture of Henri Matisse"
Gallery imprint, 22 p.
February 10 – February 28

BERGGRUEN & CIE., Paris
"Henri Matisse: papiers découpés"
Gallery imprint, 23 p.
February 27 – March 28

MINNEAPOLIS INSTITUTE OF ART
"Matisse Bronzes"
(Shown in conjunction with Klee Drawings)
From the collection of
Mr. and Mrs. Carl Frederick Hellström
July 7 – September 7

1953 NY-CARLSBERG GLYPTOTEK, Copenhagen
"Henri Matisse: Sculpturer, Malerier, Farveklip"
Museum imprint, 18 p.
(Foreword by Haavard Rostrup;
Introduction by Jean Cassou)
November 6 – December 6

1954 NATIONAL GALLERY OF CANADA, Ottawa
"Henri Matisse: Sculptures, Paintings, Drawings"
Museum imprint, 13 p.
(Introduction by Jean Cassou)
Shown previously at Tate Gallery, London

BERGGRUEN & CIE., Paris
"Henri Matisse: Lithographies rares"
Gallery imprint, 4 p.
October – November

KUNSTNERNES HUS, Oslo
"Henri Matisse"
Gallery imprint, 15 p.
(Introduction by Jean Cassou;
Foreword by Haavard Rostrup)
February 20 – March 7

MAURICE BRIDEL et NANE CAILLER, Lausanne
"Exposition de Lithographies de Matisse"
March 8 – March 27

PAUL ROSENBERG & CO., New York
"Loan Exhibition of Paintings by Henri Matisse"
Gallery imprint, 24 p.
April 5 – May 1

BOYMANS MUSEUM, Rotterdam
"Matisse: Bronzen, Tekeningen, Schilderijen, Schetsen"
Museum imprint, 15 p.
(Introduction in French and Dutch by Jean Cassou)
April 16 – June 8

XXVII ESPOSIZIONE BIENNALE
INTERNAZIONALE D'ARTE, Venice
French Pavillion – 6 works by Henri Matisse
June 19 – October 17

1954-55 CHALETTE GALLERY, New York
"Henri Matisse: Lithographs, Linoleum cuts,
Aquatints, 1925-53"
Gallery imprint, 23 p.
December 1 – January 3

1955 WINNIPEG ART GALLERY, Winnipeg, Canada
"Henri Matisse"
January 2 – January 23

JEHANGIR ART GALLERY, Bombay
"Henri Matisse"
(7th in the series – "This is Modern Art")
March 25 – April 3

THE MUSEUM OF MODERN ART, New York
"Etchings by Henri Matisse"
New York: Simon & Schuster distributors, 23 p.
(Introduction by William S. Lieberman)
May 4 – May 31

BUSCH-REISINGER MUSEUM, Harvard University,
Cambridge, Massachusetts
"Matisse" – Gallery imprint, 12 p.
(A museum course exhibition)
May 9 – June 8

MUSEUM OF FINE ARTS, Houston
"Matisse - Sculptures, Paintings, Drawings"
Gallery imprint, 13 p.
(Introduction by Jean Cassou)
September 18 – October 16

1955-56 THE MUSEUM OF MODERN ART, New York
"Matisse's Chasubles" – No publication
December 20 – January 15

1956 PETER DEITSCH GALLERY, New York
"Henri Matisse Lithographs, Drawings and Etchings".
March 2 – April 7

THE MUSEUM OF MODERN ART, New York
"Prints of Henri Matisse" – No publication.
June 27 – October 14

MUSÉE NATIONAL D'ART MODERNE, Paris
"Henri Matisse: Exposition rétrospective"
Paris: Editions des Musées Nationaux, 1956, 35 p.
(Introduction by Jean Cassou)
July 28 – November 18

1957 NATIONAL MUSEUM, Stockholm
"Henri Matisse: Apollon"
Museum imprint, 18 p. (In Swedish and French)
Apollon et sculptures
(Introduction by Bo Wennberg)
September 4 – September 23

1958 GALLERIA DEL L'OBELISCO, Rome
"Henri Matisse and Henry Moore"
January 25 – February 3

GALERIE GÉRALD CRAMER, Geneva
"Henri Matisse – Eaux-Fortes, Dessins"
February 18 – March 13

EXPOSITION UNIVERSELLE ET INTERNATIONALE
DE BRUXELLES:
50 Ans d'Art Moderne (7 paintings by Matisse,
5 from the U.S.S.R.)
April – July

BERNHEIM-JEUNE DAUBERVILLE, Paris
"Chefs-d'Oeuvre de Henri Matisse"
Gallery imprint, 22 p.
(Introduction by J. & H. Dauberville:
"Une visite à Matisse, 1942")
May – July

BERGGRUEN & CIE., Paris (cat. nr. 26)
"Henri Matisse, Dessins et sculptures inédites"
Gallery imprint, 4 p.
June

HANOVER GALLERY, London
"Giacometti, Marini, Matisse, Moore"
Gallery imprint, 24 p.
June 24 – September 13

SOCIÉTÉ ROYALE DES BEAUX-ARTS, Liège
"Léger, Matisse, Picasso, Miró, Laurens, Magnelli,
Arp, Hartung, Jacobsen"
Museum book, 225 p.
(Introduction by Jules Bosmant on Matisse)
July – September

1958 GALLERIA DEL NAVIGLIO, Milan
"Opera grafica: Braque, Matisse, Picasso"
(Cat. v. I nr. 274, 1957/58)
September 2 – September 30

FINE ARTS ASSOCIATES, New York
Sculpture and drawings
Imprint, 12 p.
(Introduction by Jean Cassou)
November 25 – December 20

1958   PIERRE MATISSE GALLERY, New York
"Matisse – Drawings and Sculpture"
December 2 – December 27

1959   NEW ART CENTER, New York
"Matisse, Villon, Pascin"
January 19 – January 31

BAYER GALLERY, New York
"Henri Matisse Drawings & Lithographs 1905-1945"
(Included unpublished photographs
of Matisse at work)
March 9 – April 11

KUNSTHAUS, Zurich
"Henri Matisse, Das Plastische Werk"
Gallery imprint, 42 p.
(Introduction by Eduard Hüttinger:
"Henri Matisse als Plastiker"; and Ulf Linde: "Apollon")
July 14 – August 12

KUNSTHALLE, Bern
"Henri Matisse 1950-54:
Les grandes gouaches découpées"
Gallery imprint, 14 p.
(Introduction by Franz Meyer)
July 25 – September 20

1959-60   GALERIE GÉRALD CRAMER, Geneva
"Le Livre Illustré par Henri Matisse:
Dessins, Documents"
Gallery imprint, 32 p.
December 4 – January 29

1960   DER WÜRTTEMBERGISCHE KUNSTVEREIN,
Stuttgart
"Französische Zeichnungen des XX. Jahrhunderts"
January 24 – February 28

1960   STEDELIJK MUSEUM, Amsterdam
"Matisse: Les grandes gouaches découpées"
Museum imprint, 13 p.
(Introduction by Franz Meyer)
April 29 – June 30

THE MUSEUM OF MODERN ART, New York
"*Jazz* by Henri Matisse"
June 17 – September 19

PAVILLON DE VENDÔME, Aix-en-Provence
"Matisse" – Gallery imprint, 38 p.
July 9 – August 31

KUNSTHAUS, Zurich
The Thompson Collection
(4 paintings by Matisse, 5 gouaches découpées)
October – November

1960-61   MUSÉE D'ART MODERNE, Paris
"Les Sources du XXᵉ siècle"
November – January

KLIPSTEIN & CIE (Kornfeld), Bern
"Henri Matisse, Das illustrierte Werk,
Zeichnungen und Druckgraphik"
Gallery imprint, 47 p.
December 15 – January 31

1961   MUSÉE DES ARTS DÉCORATIFS, Paris
"Henri Matisse: Les grandes gouaches découpées"
Museum imprint, 74 p.
(Introduction by Jacques Lassaigne)
March 22 – May 14

1961   MUSÉE TOULOUSE-LAUTREC, Albi
"Henri Matisse" Museum imprint, 72 p.
(Introduction by Jacques Lassaigne:
"Hommage à Matisse")
July 11 – September 15

THE MUSEUM OF MODERN ART, New York
"The last works of Henri Matisse, large cut gouaches"
Introduction by Monroe Wheeler
New York: Doubleday, Garden City, 47 p.
October 17 – December 3

Also shown:
THE ART INSTITUTE OF CHICAGO
January 10 – February 13

SAN FRANCISCO MUSEUM OF ART
March 12 – April 22

1962   GALERIE CHARPENTIER, Paris
"Les Fauves"
March 7 – June 15

HANOVER GALLERY, London
"Matisse, Modigliani, Drawings"
March 21 – April 19

PETER DEITSCH GALLERY, New York
"Henri Matisse Etchings"
All executed in 1929
April 10 – April 28

1963   Inauguration of the MUSÉE MATISE
in the Villa des Arènes in Cimiez-Nice.
Inaugurated by Gaetan Picon and Jean Cassou
in the presence of Mᵐᵉ Georges Duthuit,
Jean Matisse and Pierre Matisse
January 5

GALERIE JACQUES DUBOURG, Paris
"Henri Matisse, Aquarelles, Dessins"
(With "Notes sur la Couleur" by Henri Matisse)
Gallery imprint, 21 p.
June

1964   GALERIE ADRIEN MAEGHT, Paris
"Henri Matisse, Gravures"
June – July

DOCUMENTA III – Kassel
(6 paintings, 13 drawings, and sculpture)
June – October

CHAMBRE DE COMMERCE, Saint-Quentin
Exhibition of Students and Former Students
of the Ecole de la Tour (16 drawings by Matisse)

PALAIS DE BEAULIEU, Lausanne
"Masterpieces from Swiss Collections"
Manet to Picasso (7 paintings by Matisse)
Exhibition at Lausanne Fair
May 1 – October 25

FRANK PERLS GALLERY, Beverly Hills
"Matisse – Picasso"
Drawings and Graphic Work
Gallery imprint, one reproduction
December

1965   P. N. MATISSE, Beverly Hills
Matisse drawings (18)
Gallery imprint, one reproduction
April – May

Catalogue of the HENRI MATISSE RETROSPECTIVE of 1966

All dates and titles for the Henri Matisse
retrospective of 1966 *have been provided by
the three children of Matisse, Madame Georges Duthuit,
Jean Matisse and Pierre Matisse, from the material
in their extensive files and their own personal recollections.
Additional titles listed have been in common usage.
In all dimension references, height precedes width;
all dimensions are given in inches.
Dates printed in parentheses do not appear on the work.
An asterisk (*) in front of the number indicates
the work is reproduced within these pages.*

PAINTINGS

*1   Books and Candle   1890

Nature morte aux livres
15 × 18⅛″   Signed and dated lower left
Jean Matisse, Paris
Exhibited:
1920 *Henri Matisse*, Galerie Bernheim-Jeune,
      Paris. No. 2
1949 *Henri Matisse*, Musée des Beaux-Arts,
      Lucerne. No. 1
1951-52 *Henri Matisse*, The Museum of Modern
      Art, New York; The Cleveland Museum
      of Art; The Art Institute of Chicago;
      The San Francisco Museum of Art. No. 1
1952 *Henri Matisse*, The Los Angeles Municipal
      Art Department, arranged by The Museum
      of Modern Art, New York. No. 1

*2   Interior with a Top Hat   (1896)

*Intérieur au chapeau; Nature morte au chapeau
haut-de-forme*
31½ × 37⅜″   Signed lower right
Monsieur and Madame Georges Duthuit, Paris
Exhibited:
1950 *Henri Matisse*, Maison de la Pensée
      Française, Paris. No. 33

*3   Still Life   (1896)

Nature morte à l'auto-portrait
25½ × 32″   Signed lower left
Sam Salz, New York
Exhibited:
1908 Galerie Bernheim-Jeune, Paris

*4   Breton Serving Girl   1896

La desserte; Servante bretonne; La serveuse bretonne
35½ × 29½′   Signed and dated lower left
Private Collection, Paris
Exhibited:
1949 *Henri Matisse*, Musée des Beaux-Arts,
      Lucerne. No. 10
1950 *Henri Matisse*, Galerie des Ponchettes,
      Nice. No. 4
1950 *XXV Biennale di Venezia*, Venice. No. 25
1951-52 *Henri Matisse*, The Museum of Modern
      Art, New York; The Cleveland Museum
      Art; The Art Institute of Chicago; The
      San Francisco Museum of Art. No. 2
1952 *Henri Matisse*, The Los Angeles Municipal
      Art Department, arranged by The
      Museum of Modern Art, New York. No.

*5   Courtyard of a Farm in Brittany   1897

Cour de ferme bretonne
12¾ × 16″   Signed and dated lower right
Private Collection, Paris

*6   Still Life   (1898)

Nature morte
15 × 18″   Signed lower left
Private Collection, Paris

*7   Peach Trees in Bloom   1899

Les pêchers en fleur
13½ × 18¼″   Signed and dated lower right
Private Collection, Paris

All paintings are oil on canvas unless otherwise noted

*8   Interior: Sideboard and Table   (1899)

Nature morte: buffet et table
25 ½ × 32 ½"   Signed lower left
Mrs. Robert Woods Bliss, Washington, D.C.
Exhibited:
   1951-52   *Henri Matisse*, The Museum of Modern
            Art, New York; The Cleveland Museum
            of Art; The Art Institute of Chicago;
            The San Francisco Museum of Art. No. 6
   1954   *Masters of Modern Art*, The Museum of
            Modern Art, New York
   1956   *Rétrospective Henri Matisse*, Musée National
            d'Art Moderne, Paris. No. 4
   1962   The San Francisco Museum of Art
   1962   The Museum of Fine Arts, Houston.

*9   Male Model   (1900)

Le serf; Harmonie bleue; Bevilacqua; Académie bleue
39⅜ × 28¾"   Not signed
Mr. and Mrs. Pierre Matisse
Exhibited:
   1946   *Matisse - Picasso*, Palais des Beaux-Arts,
            Brussels. No. 2
   1949   *Henri Matisse*, Musée des Beaux-Arts,
            Lucerne. No. 19
   1951-52   *Henri Matisse*, The Museum of Modern
            Art, New York; The Cleveland Museum of
            Art; The Art Institute of Chicago;
            The San Francisco Museum of Art. No. 6
   1952   *Henri Matisse*, The Los Angeles Municipal
            Art Department, arranged by The Museum
            of Modern Art, New York. No. 5

*10   Self Portrait   (1900)

Auto-portrait
25³/₁₆ × 17¾"   Signed lower left
Monsieur and Madame Georges Duthuit, Paris
Exhibited:
   1949   *Henri Matisse*, Musée des Beaux-Arts,
            Lucerne. No. 17
   1962   *Cent ans de portrait*, Galerie Bernheim-Jeune,
            Paris. No. 36
   1963   *Das französische Portrait im XX. Jahrhundert*,
            Kunsthalle, Düsseldorf; Akademie der Künste
            Berlin

*11   The Seine   (1900-01)

La Seine
23 × 28"   Signed lower left
Wright Saltus Ludington, Santa Barbara, California
Exhibited:
   1964   *From The Ludington Collection*, Dickson Art
            Center, University of California, Los
            Angeles. No. 26

*12   Japanese Lady (Madame Matisse)   (1901)

La Japonaise
46 × 31 ½"   Not signed
Private Collection, Paris
Exhibited:
   1949   *Henri Matisse*, Musée des Beaux-Arts,
            Lucerne. No. 27
   1952   *Henri Matisse*, Knokke-le-Zoute

*13   Standing Nude   (1901)

Nu debout
31 ½ × 23 ¼"   Signed lower right

Mr. and Mrs. Gifford Phillips, Santa Monica,
California
Exhibited:
   1962   *Gifford and Joann Phillips Collection*, Dickson
            Art Center, University of California,
            Los Angeles

*14   A Glimpse of Notre Dame in the Late Afternoon
1902

Notre-Dame, une fin d'après-midi
28 ½ × 21 ½"   Signed and dated lower left
Albright-Knox Art Gallery, Buffalo, New York,
Seymour H. Knox Fund
Exhibited:
   1931   *Henri Matisse*, The Museum of Modern Art,
            New York
   1934   University of Rochester, New York
   1936-38   *20th Century European Painting*, Boyer
            Galleries, Philadelphia; The Art Gallery
            of Toronto, Ontario
   1941   *Fauve Exhibition*, Marie Harriman Gallery,
            New York
   1943   *Henri Matisse Retrospective Exhibition of
            Paintings, 1898-1939*, Pierre Matisse Gallery,
            New York. No. 3
   1947   *Symbolism and Poetic Painting*, The Museum
            of Modern Art, New York
   1951   *Paris as Seen by Painters*, The Museum of Art,
            Rhode Island School of Design,
            Providence. No. 14
   1952   *Art and City Life*, The Columbus Gallery
            of Fine Arts, Ohio
   1955   *Matisse Sculptures, Paintings and Drawings*,
            The Museum of Fine Arts, Houston. No. 62
   1959   *Les Fauves*, The Dallas Museum for
            Contemporary Arts. No. 24
   1960-61   *Les sources du XXᵉ siècle (Les arts en Europe,
            de 1884-1914)*   Musée National d'Art
            Moderne, Paris. No. 428
   1961   *Paintings and Sculpture from the Albright
            Art Gallery*, Yale University Art Gallery,
            New Haven. No. 47

*15   Guitarist (Madame Matisse)   (1903)

Guitariste
21 ½ × 15"   Signed lower right
Mr. and Mrs. Ralph F. Colin, New York
Exhibited:
   1926   *Henri Matisse*, Galeries Georges Petit, Paris
   1950   *Works of Art Belonging to Alumnae*, Smith
            College Museum of Art, Northampton,
            Mass. No. 59
   1950   *The Eye Listens—Music in the Visual Arts*,
            Dwight Art Memorial, Mount Holyoke
            College, South Hadley, Mass. No. 70
   1951-52   *Henri Matisse*, The Museum of Modern
            Art, New York; The Cleveland Museum
            of Art; The Art Institute of Chicago;
            The San Francisco Museum of Art. No. 9
   1952   *Henri Matisse*, The Los Angeles Municipal
            Art Department, arranged by the Museum
            of Modern Art, New York. No. 6
   1955   *Paintings from Private Collections*, The Museum
            of Modern Art, New York. No. 14
   1956   *Rétrospective Henri Matisse*, Musée National
            d'Art Moderne, Paris. No. 10
   1959   *Les Fauves*, Dallas Museum for Contemporary
            Arts. No. 26
   1960   *The Colin Collection*, M. Knoedler & Co., Inc.,
            New York. No. 16

*16 Carmelina (1903)

32 × 23½″   Signed lower left
Museum of Fine Arts, Boston
Exhibited:
1912 *Second Post-Impressionist Exhibition*, Grafton
 Galleries, London. No. 9
1931 *Henri Matisse*, Galeries Georges Petit. No. 7bis
1931 *Henri Matisse*, The Museum of Modern Art,
 New York. No. 8
1931 *Henri Matisse*, The Museum of Art, Rhode
 Island School of Design, Providence. No. 5
1937 Fogg Art Museum, Harvard University,
 Cambridge
1946 *Nude in Art*, Wadsworth Atheneum,
 Hartford. No. 36
1946-47 *Development of French Culture for 200 Years*,
 The Museum of Art, Toledo, Ohio;
 The Toronto Art Gallery, Toronto, Ontario
1948 *Henri Matisse Retrospective*, The Philadelphia
 Museum of Art. No. 9
1951-52 *Henri Matisse*, The Museum of Modern
 Art, New York; The Cleveland Museum
 of Art; The Art Institute of Chicago;
 The San Francisco Museum of Art. No. 8
1956 *Rétrospective Henri Matisse*, Musée National
 d'Art Moderne, Paris. No. 9
1964 *The Nude in Art*, Vancouver Art Gallery,
 B.C. No. 79

*17 St. Anne's Chapel (1904)

La Chapelle Sainte-Anne
23⅝ × 28¾″   Signed lower right
Mr. and Mrs. Pierre Matisse

*18 Woman with the Hat (1904-05)

Femme au chapeau; Madame Matisse
32 × 23½″   Signed upper left
Mr. and Mrs. Walter A. Haas, San Francisco
Exhibited:
1905 Salon des Indépendants, Paris
1951-52 *Henri Matisse*, The Museum of Modern
 Art, New York; The Cleveland Museum
 of Art; The Art Institute of Chicago;
 The San Francisco Museum of Art. No. 13
1953 *Les Fauves*, The San Francisco Museum of Art
1955 *Art in the 20th Century*, The San Francisco
 Museum of Art
1959 *Signposts of XXth Century Art*, The Dallas
 Museum for Contemporary Arts
1960 *Modern Masters in West Coast Collections*, The
 San Francisco Museum of Art
1962 The San Francisco Museum of Art
1962 The Museum of Contemporary Art, Houston
1965 *Man, Glory, Jest and Riddle*, The San
 Francisco Museum of Art

*19 Woman with Parasol (1905)

Femme à l'ombrelle
18¹/₁₆ × 14¾″   Signed lower right
Musée Matisse, Cimiez—Nice
Exhibited:
1952 *Henri Matisse*, Knokke-le-Zoute

*20 The Port of Abaill, Collioure (1905)

Le Port d'Abaill
23⅝ × 58¼″   Not signed
Jean Matisse, Paris

Exhibited:
1961 *Henri Matisse*, Musée Toulouse-Lautrec,
 Palais de la Berbie, Albi, France. No. 4
1962 *Les Fauves*, Galerie Charpentier, Paris. No.

*21 Pastoral (1906)

Pastorale
18⅛ × 21¾″   Not signed
Musée d'Art Moderne de la Ville de Paris
Exhibited:
1931 *Henri Matisse*, The Museum of Modern Art,
 New York. No. 11
1950 *Autour de 1900*, Galerie Charpentier, Paris
1951 *Œuvres choisies du XXᵉ siècle*, Galerie
 Kaganovich, Paris
1954 *La Collection Girardin*, Musée d'Art Moderne
 de la Ville de Paris
1956 *Rétrospective Henri Matisse*, Musée National
 d'Art Moderne, Paris. No. 16
1958 *50 Ans d'Art Moderne*, Palais International
 des Beaux-Arts, Universal and International
 Exhibition, Brussels

*22 Reading (1906)

La lecture; Intérieur à la fillette
29½ × 24½″   Signed lower left
Mr. and Mrs. William Goetz, Los Angeles
Exhibited:
1906 *Henri Matisse*, Galerie Druet, Paris
1952 *Some Business Men Collect Contemporary Art*,
 Dallas Museum of Fine Arts
1952 *Henri Matisse*, Frank Perls Gallery, Beverly
 Hills
1952 *Henri Matisse*, The Los Angeles Municipal
 Art Department, arranged by The Museum
 of Modern Art, New York. No. 8
1952-53 *Les Fauves*, The Museum of Modern Art,
 New York; The Minneapolis Institute
 of Arts; The San Francisco Museum of Art;
 The Art Gallery of Toronto, Ontario
1959 *The Collection of Mr. and Mrs. William Goetz*,
 The California Palace of the Legion
 of Honor, San Francisco

*23 Still Life with Geranium Plant and Fruit (1906

Nature morte au géranium
38½ × 31½″   Signed lower left
The Art Institute of Chicago,
The Joseph Winterbotham Collection
Exhibited:
1929 *French Painting of the 19th and 20th Centuries*,
 The Fogg Art Museum, Harvard
 University, Cambridge. No. 61
1938 *Twenty Oils by Henri Matisse*, The Cleveland
 Museum of Art
1940 *Isms and How They Grew*, The Baltimore
 Museum of Art
1941 *From Cézanne to Picasso*, The Los Angeles
 County Museum of Art. No. 28
1941 *Fauve Exhibition*, Marie Harriman Gallery,
 New York
1945 *Masterpieces of European and American Art*
 (Lent by The Art Institute of Chicago)
 Decatur Art Center; Springfied Art
 Association, Ill. No. 10
1945 *Flower Painting*, Milwaukee Art Institute.
 No. 22
1948 *Henri Matisse Retrospective*, The Philadelph
 Museum of Art. No. 19

1948-49 *Nineteenth Century French Paintings,*
Saginaw Museum, Michigan. No. 18

1949 Dallas Museum of Fine Arts

1950 *Les Fauves,* Sidney Janis Gallery, New York.
No. 32

1951-52 *Henri Matisse,* The Museum of Modern
Art, New York; The Cleveland Museum
of Art; The Art Institute of Chicago;
The San Francisco Museum of Art. No. 14

1954 *Ten Directions by Ten Artists,* Denver
Art Museum. No. 37

1956 *Les Fauves,* The Arts Club of Chicago. No. 12

1956 *25th Anniversary Exhibition,* Joslyn Art Center,
Omaha, Nebraska

*24   The Young Sailor, II   1906

Jeune marin à la casquette; Le jeune marin, II
39⅜×31⅞″   Signed and dated lower left
Mr. and Mrs. Leigh B. Block, Chicago
Exhibited:

1912 *Sonderbund* Cologne. p. 149

1912 *Second Post-Impressionist Exhibition,*
Grafton Galleries, London

1913 *The Armory Show,* New York City. No. 405

1913 *International Exhibition of Modern Art,*
The Art Institute of Chicago

1915 *Henri Matisse,* Montross Gallery, New York

1931 *Henri Matisse,* Kunsthalle, Basel

1931 *Henri Matisse,* The Museum of Modern Art,
New York. No. 14

1948 *Henri Matisse Retrospective,* The Philadelphia
Museum of Art. No. 10

1949 *Henri Matisse,* Musée des Beaux-Arts,
Lucerne. No. 34

1950 *I "Fauves",* XXV Biennale di Venezia,
Venice. No. 45

1951-52 *Henri Matisse,* The Museum of Modern
Art, New York; The Cleveland Museum
of Art; The Art Institute of Chicago;
The San Francisco Museum of Art. No. 15

*25   Music (Sketch)   (1907)

La musique (esquisse)
29×24″   Signed lower left
The Museum of Modern Art, New York, gift
of A. Conger Goodyear in honor of Alfred H. Barr Jr.
Exhibited:

1907 *Salon d'Automne,* Paris; traveling to London.
Berlin, Stockholm, New York and Moscow

1910 *Henri Matisse,* Bernheim-Jeune, Paris

1931 *Henri Matisse,* The Museum of Modern Art,
New York. No. 16

1934 *French Painting from 15th Century to Present Day,*
The California Palace of the Legion of
Honor, San Francisco

1934 *Modern Works of Art,* Fifth Anniversary
Exhibition, The Museum of Modern Art,
New York

1936 *La Danse,* Pierre Matisse Gallery New York

1948 *Henri Matisse Retrospective,* The Philadelphia
Museum of Art. No. 18

1951-52 *Henri Matisse,* The Museum of Modern
Art, New York; The Cleveland Museum
of Art; The Art Institute of Chicago;
The San Francisco Museum of Art. No. 17

1952 *Henri Matisse,* The Los Angeles Municipal
Art Department, arranged by The Museum
of Modern Art, New York. No. 9

1955 *Paintings from Private Collections,* The Museum
of Modern Art, New York

1965 *Recent Acquisitions: Painting and Sculpture,*
The Museum of Modern Art, New York

*26   Bathers with a Turtle; Women by the Sea   1908

Baigneuse à la tortue
70½×86¾″   Signed and dated lower right
City Art Museum of Saint Louis, gift of Mr. and
Mrs. Joseph Pulitzer, Jr.
Exhibited:

1931 *Henri Matisse,* Kunsthalle, Basel. No. 143

1931 *Henri Matisse,* The Museum of Modern Art,
New York. No. 17

1940 *Modern Paintings,* Pierre Matisse Gallery
New York

1947 *A St. Louis Private Collection,* The City Art
Museum of St. Louis.

1948 *Henri Matisse Retrospective,* The Philadelphia
Museum of Art. No. 17

1951-52 *Henri Matisse,* The Museum of Modern
Art, New York; The Cleveland Museum
of Art; The Art Institute of Chicago;
The San Francisco Museum of Art. No. 18

1952 *Henri Matisse,* The Los Angeles Municipal
Art Department, arranged by The Museum
of Modern Art, New York. No. 10

1953 *Matisse,* Society of the Four Arts, Palm Beach,
Florida

1955 *The Arts of Matisse,* Busch-Reisinger Museum,
Cambridge

1956 *Rétrospective Henri Matisse,* Musée National
d'Art Moderne, Paris. No. 24

1957 *Modern Painting, Drawing and Sculpture*
(collected by Louise and Joseph Pulitzer, Jr.),
M. Knoedler and Co., Inc., New York;
The Fogg Art Museum, Harvard University,
Cambridge

1961 *Works of Art from the Collections of the Harvard
Class of 1936,* Fogg Art Museum, Harvard
University, Cambridge

*27   Girl with Green Eyes   (1909)

La femme aux yeux verts
26×20″   Signed lower right
The San Francisco Museum of Art, bequest
of Harriet Lane Levy
Exhibited:

1931 *Henri Matisse,* The Museum of Modern Art,
New York. No. 19b

1934 *French Painting from 15th Century to Present Day,*
The California Palace of the Legion
of Honor, San Francisco. No. 203

1936 *Henri Matisse 1889-1936,* The San Francisco
Museum of Art

1951-52 *Henri Matisse,* The Museum of Modern
Art, New York; The Cleveland Museum
of Art; The Art Institute of Chicago;
The San Francisco Museum of Art. No. 22

1952 *Henri Matisse,* The Los Angeles Municipal
Art Department, arranged by the Museum
of Modern Art, New York. No. 13

1953 *Les Fauves,* The San Francisco Museum of Art

1955 *Art of the 20th Century,* The San Francisco
Museum of Art

1956 *Les Fauves,* The Arts Club of Chicago

1956 *Rétrospective Henri Matisse,* Musée National
d'Art Moderne, Paris. No. 27

1961 *The Logic of Modern Art,* William Rockhill
Nelson Gallery of Art and Mary Atkins
Museum of Fine Arts, Kansas City, Mo.

*28   Pierre Matisse   (1909)

16×13″   Not signed
Private Collection, New York

Exhibited:

1945 *Henri Matisse*, Wildenstein Gallery. No. 46
1948 *Henri Matisse Retrospective*, The Philadelphia Museum of Art. No. 11
1951-52 *Henri Matisse*, The Museum of Modern Art, New York; The Cleveland Museum of Art; The Art Institute of Chicago; The San Francisco Museum of Art. No. 21
1952 *Henri Matisse*, The Los Angeles Municipal Art Department, arranged by The Museum of Modern Art, New York. No. 12
1959 *Les Fauves*, Dallas Museum for Contemporary Arts. No. 27

*29   Dance (first version)   (1909)

La danse—esquisse
102½ × 153½″   Not signed
The Museum of Modern Art, New York, gift of Nelson A. Rockefeller in honor of Alfred H. Barr, Jr.
Exhibited:

1912 *Second Post-Impressionist Exhibition*, Grafton Galleries, London. No. 185
1912 *Sezession*, Berlin
1936 *La Danse*, Pierre Matisse Gallery, New York
1939 *Art in Our Time*, The Museum of Modern Art, New York. No. 91
1940 *Origins of Modern Art*, The Arts Club of Chicago. No. 41
1941 *Collection of Walter P. Chrysler, Jr.*, The Virginia Museum of Fine Arts, Richmond; The Philadelphia Museum of Art. No 117
1948 *Henri Matisse Retrospective*, The Philadelphia Museum of Art. No. 20
1951-52 *Henri Matisse*, The Museum of Modern Art, New York; The Cleveland Museum of Art; The Art Institute of Chicago; The San Francisco Museum of Art. No. 20
1952 *Henri Matisse*, The Portland Art Museum, Oregon, arranged by The Museum of Modern Art, New York
1956-57 *Paintings from the Collection of Walter P. Chrysler, Jr.*, Portland Art Museum, Oregon (circulating). No. 93
1960 *French Paintings, 1789-1929, From the Collection of Walter P. Chrysler, Jr.*, The Dayton Art Institute, Ohio. No. 117

*30   Girl with a Black Cat (Marguerite Matisse)   1910

Jeune fille au chat noir (Marguerite Matisse)
37 × 25¼″   Signed and dated lower right
Monsieur and Madame Georges Duthuit, Paris
Exhibited:

1913 *The Armory Show*, New York City. No. 408
1931 *Henri Matisse*, Galeries Georges Petit. No. 23
1931 *Henri Matisse*, The Museum of Modern Art, New York. No. 20
1931 *Henri Matisse*, Kunsthalle, Basel
1948 *Henri Matisse Retrospective*, The Philadelphia Museum of Art. No. 21
1949 *Henri Matisse*, Musée des Beaux-Arts, Lucerne. No. 38
1951-52 *Henri Matisse*, The Museum of Modern Art, New York; The Cleveland Museum of Art; The Art Institute of Chicago; The San Francisco Museum of Art. No. 24
1952 *Henri Matisse*, The Los Angeles Municipal Art Department, arranged by the Museum of Modern Art, New York. No. 15
1956 *Rétrospective Henri Matisse*, Musée National d'Art Moderne, Paris. No. 24
1960 *Matisse*, Pavillon de Vendôme, Aix-en-Provence. No 10

*31   The Blue Window   (1911)

La fenêtre bleue
51½ × 35⅝″   Signed lower left
The Museum of Modern Art, New York, Abby Aldrich Rockefeller Fund
Exhibited:

1939 *Art in Our Time: 10th Anniversary Exhibition*, The Museum of Modern Art, New York. No. 93
1941 *Paintings Expelled from German Museums*, Lawrence Art Museum, Williams College, Williamstown, Mass.
1943 *Matisse Retrospective*, Pierre Matisse Gallery, New York
1944 *Art in Progress: 15th Anniversary Exhibition*, Museum of Modern Art, New York
1948 *Henri Matisse Retrospective*, The Philadelphia Museum of Art. No. 25
1951-52 *Henri Matisse*, The Museum of Modern Art, New York; The Cleveland Museum of Art; The Art Institute of Chicago; The San Francisco Museum of Art. No. 28
1952 *Henri Matisse*, The Los Angeles Municipal Department, arranged by The Museum of Modern Art, New York. No. 19
1954 *Curt Valentin Memorial Exhibition*, Curt Valentin Gallery, New York
1955 *XXV Anniversary Exhibition*, The Museum of Modern Art, New York
1956 *Rétrospective Henri Matisse*, Musée National d'Art Moderne, Paris. No. 31
1957 *Verkannte Kunst*, Staedtische Kunsthalle, Recklinghausen
1962 *Sonderbund*, Wallraf-Richartz Museum, Cologne
1963-64 *Paintings from The Museum of Modern Art, New York*, The National Gallery of Art, Washington, D.C.

*32   Zorah in Yellow   (1912)

La robe jaune
32 × 25″   Signed lower left
Mr. and Mrs. Alfred Cowles, Lake Forest, Illinois
Exhibited:

1951-52 *Henri Matisse*, The Museum of Modern Art, New York; The Cleveland Museum of Art; The Art Institute of Chicago; The San Francisco Museum of Art. No. 31
1952 *Henri Matisse*, The Los Angeles Municipal Department arranged by the Museum of Modern Art, New York. No. 21
1961 *Treasures of Chicago Collections*, The Art Institute of Chicago

*33   Oranges (Tangier)   (1912)

Nature morte aux oranges
37 × 33⅛″   Not signed
Monsieur and Madame Pablo Picasso, Mougins, France
Exhibited:

1956 *Rétrospective Henri Matisse*, Musée National d'Art Moderne, Paris. No. 33

*34   Open Window, Tangier   (1913)

La fenêtre ouverte
59½ × 37″   Not signed
Private Collection, Paris
Exhibited:

1960 *Matisse*, Pavillon de Vendôme, Aix-en-Provence. No. 11

*35 Mademoiselle Yvonne Landsberg 1914
58 × 38½″   Signed and dated lower left
The Philadelphia Museum of Art, The Louise and
Walter Arensberg Collection
Exhibited:
1915   *Henri Matisse*, Montross Gallery, New York
       City. No. 62
1934   *French Painting*, The California Palace of the
       Legion of Honor, San Francisco. No. 204
1942   *20th Century Portraits*, The Museum of Modern
       Art, New York. p. 55
1948   *Henri Matisse Retrospective*, The Philadelphia
       Museum of Art, No. 28
1948   *Modern Artists in Transition*, Opening Exhibition
       of The Modern Institute of Art, Beverly Hills.
       No. 16
1949   *Arensberg Collection*, The Art Institute of
       Chicago. No. 137
1951-52 *Henri Matisse*, The Museum of Modern Art,
       New York; The Cleveland Museum of Art;
       The Art Institute of Chicago;
       The San Francisco Museum of Art. No. 34a
1954   *Arensberg Collection*, The Philadelphia Museum
       of Art. No. 133
1956   *Rétrospective Henri Matisse*, Musée National
       d'Art Moderne, Paris. No. 35
1957   *European Masters*, Boston Museum of Fine Arts.
1961   *Arensberg and Gallatin Collections*, The
       Guggenheim Museum, New York
1964   *Exhibition 1914*, The Baltimore Museum of
       Art. No. 153

*36 Open Window, Collioure   (1914)
La porte-fenêtre
46″ × 35½″   Not signed
Monsieur and Madame Georges Duthuit, Paris

*37 View of Notre-Dame   (1914)
Une vue de Notre-Dame
57¾ × 37″   Signed lower left
Private Collection, New York
Exhibited:
1949   *Henri Matisse*, Musée des Beaux-Arts, Lucerne.
       No. 43

*38 Lilac Branch   1914
La branche de lilas
57 × 38″   Signed and dated lower right
Private Collection, New York

*39 Portrait of Madame Greta Prozor   (1916)
57½ × 37¾″   Not signed
Private Collection, New Nork
Exhibited:
1949   *Henri Matisse*, Musée des Beaux-Arts, Lucerne.
       No. 46

*40 Marguerite Matisse with Black Velvet Ribbon   (1916)
Marguerite Matisse au ruban noir de velours
7¼ × 6¾″   Signed lower right
Private Collection, Paris

*41 Studio, Quai St. Michel   (1916)
L'atelier, Quai Saint-Michel
57½ × 45¾″   Not signed
The Phillips Collection, Washington, D.C.

Exhibited:
1931   *Henri Matisse*, Galeries Georges Petit, Paris.
       No. 36
1931   *Henri Matisse*, The Museum of Modern Art,
       New York. No. 35
1940-41 *Henri Matisse*, Pierre Matisse Gallery,
       New York
1948   *Henri Matisse Retrospective*, The Philadelphia
       Museum of Art. No. 34
1950   *Diamond Jubilee Exhibition*, The Philadelphia
       Museum of Art. No. 96
1951   Person Hall Art Gallery, University of North
       Carolina, Durham
1951-52 *Henri Matisse*, The Museum of Modern Art,
       New York; The Cleveland Museum
       of Art; The Art Institute of Chicago;
       The San Francisco Museum of Art. No. 44
1961   *Masterpieces*, Wildenstein & Co., New York

*42 Lorette and Aïcha   (1916)
15 × 18″   Signed lower left
Private Collection, New York

*43 The Green Robe   1916
Lorette sur fond noir; La robe verte
28¾ × 21½″   Signed and dated lower right
Mr. and Mrs. Pierre Matisse
Exhibited:
1931   *Henri Matisse*, The Museum of Modern Art,
       New York. No. 34
1949   *Henri Matisse*, Musée des Beaux-Arts, Lucerne.
       No. 48
1951-52 *Henri Matisse*, The Museum of Modern
       Art, New York; The Cleveland Museum of
       Art; The Art Institute oî Chicago;
       The San Francisco Museum of Art. No. 46
1952   *Henri Matisse*, The Los Angeles Municipal Art
       Department, arranged by The Museum of
       Modern Art, New York. No. 29
1955   *Rétrospective Henri Matisse*, Salon d'Automne,
       Paris
1956   *Rétrospective Henri Matisse*, Musée National
       d'Art Moderne, Paris. No. 44

*44 The Green Gandoura Robe   (1916)
La gandoura verte
12⅞ × 9⅜″   Signed upper left
Mr. and Mrs. Ralph F. Colin, New York
Exhibited:
1934   *Henri Matisse*, Pierre Matisse Gallery, New
       York. No. 23
1948   *Henri Matisse Retrospective*, The Philadelphia
       Museum of Art. No. 40
1948   *Some Paintings from Alumnae Collections*, Smith
       College Museum of Art, Northampton, Mass.
1951   *New York Private Collections*, The Museum of
       Modern Art, New York
1956   *Rétrospective Henri Matisse*, Musée National
       d'Art Moderne, Paris. No. 45
1960   *The Colin Collection*, M. Knoedler & Co., Inc.,
       New York. No. 17

45 Tree Near Trivaux Pond   (1916-17)
Arbre près de l'étang de Trivaux
36½ × 29¼″   Signed lower right
The Trustees of The Tate Gallery, London
Exhibited:
1923   *Modern French Paintings*, Leicester Galleries,
       London. No. 30

1931 *Henri Matisse*, Galeries Georges Petit, Paris. No. 141 bis
1933 *Re-Opening Exhibition*, Walker Art Gallery, Liverpool. No. 600
1956 *Rétrospective Henri Matisse*, Musée National d'Art Moderne, Paris. No. 41

*46 The Pewter Jug (1916-17)

Le pot d'étain
36¼ × 25⅝"　　Signed lower left
The Baltimore Museum of Art, Cone Collection
Exhibited:
1931 *Henri Matisse*, Galeries Georges Petit, Paris
1931 *Matisse*, Kunsthalle, Basel
1931 *Henri Matisse*, The Museum of Modern Art, New York. No. 44
1941 *A Century of Baltimore Collecting*, The Baltimore Museum of Art
1948 *Henri Matisse Retrospective*, The Philadelphia Museum of Art. No 30
1951-52 *Henri Matisse*, The Museum of Modern Art, New York; The Cleveland Museum of Art; The Art Institute of Chicago; The San Francisco Museum of Art. No 42
1953 *The Cone Collection*, The Virginia Museum of Fine Arts, Richmond
1955 *The Cone Collection*, M. Knoedler & Co., Inc., New York

*47 The Pewter Jug (1916-17)

Le pot d'étain
19¹¹/₁₆ × 15¾"　Oil on wood.　　Signed lower right
Professor Hans R. Hahnloser, Bern
Exhibited:
1941 *Hauptwerke der Sammlung Hahnloser*, Musée des Beaux-Arts, Lucerne. No. 69
1949 *Henri Matisse*, Musée des Beaux-Arts, Lucerne. No. 49

*48 Marguerite in a Fur Hat 1917

Marguerite au chapeau de fourrure
16⅛ × 13"　　Signed and dated lower left
Private Collection, Paris

*49 The Painter and his Model (1917)

Le peintre et son modèle
57⅞ × 38³/₁₆"　　Not signed
Musée National d'Art Moderne, Paris
Exhibited:
1945 *Trente ans d'art indépendant*, Sté des Indépendants. 1926, XIᵉ Salon d'Automne, Paris
1945 *Matisse - Picasso*, The Victoria and Albert Museum, London
1948 *Henri Matisse Retrospective*, The Philadelphia Museum of Art. No. 42
1950-51 *L'Ecole de Paris*, Royal Academy, Burlington House, London. No. 41
1952 *Cent Chefs-d'Oeuvre du Musée d'Art Moderne*, Amsterdam and Brussels
1956 *Rétrospective Henri Matisse*, Musée National d'Art Moderne, Paris. No. 50
1958 *50 Ans d'Art Moderne*, Palais International, Universal and International Exhibition, Brussels
1960 *Oeuvres de jeunesse, de maturité et de vieillesse*, Stedelijk Museum, Amsterdam

*50 Self Portrait (1918)

Auto-portrait
23⅝ × 21¼"　　Signed lower right
Jean Matisse, Paris
Exhibited:
1951-52 *Henri Matisse*, The Museum of Modern A New York; The Cleveland Museum of A The Art Institute of Chicago; The San Francisco Museum of Art. No. 48
1952 *Henri Matisse*, The Los Angeles Municipal Department, arranged by the Museum of Modern Art, New York. No. 30
1960 *Matisse*, Pavillon de Vendôme, Aix-en-Provence. No 16
1961 *Rétrospective Henri Matisse*, Musée Toulouse Lautrec, Palais de la Berbie, Albi, France No. 7

*51 White Plumes (1919)

Les plumes blanches
27⁹/₁₆ × 23¹³/₁₆"　　Signed upper right
The Gothenburg Art Gallery, Sweden
Exhibited:
1954 *Cézanne till Picasso* (From Cézanne to Pica French Art in Swedish possession), Liljeva Konsthall, Stockholm. No. 242

*52 The Artist and his Model (1919)

L'artiste et son modèle
23½ × 28"　　Signed lower right
Dr. and Mrs. Harry Bakwin, New York
Exhibited:
1946 The Museum of Modern Art, New York
1953 Paul Rosenberg and Co., New York
1953-55 The Museum of Modern Art, New York, Circulating Exhibition
1962 *Masterpieces*, Wildenstein & Co., New Yor

*53 Girl Reading (1920)

Liseuse
10⅝ × 13¾"　　Signed lower right
Pierre Lévy, Troyes, France
Exhibited:
1949 Musée des Beaux-Arts, Palais Saint-Pierre Lyon.
1949 Kunstmuseum, Lucerne
1950 *Henri Matisse*, Galerie des Ponchettes, Nic
1955 *Réalités et Poésie ou La joie de peindre*, Galer Romanet, Paris
1957 Galerie des Ponchettes, Nice
1958 *Henri Matisse*, Galerie Bernheim-Jeune Dauberville, Paris. No. 28
1961 *Aspect de la peinture française de Courbet à So* Musée Baron Martin, Gray, France. No.
1962 *Gustave Moreau & ses élèves*, Musée Cantini Marseille. No. 78
1965 *Quarante tableaux d'une collection privée*, M. Knoedler & Cⁱᵉ, Paris. No. 23

*54 Woman with the Hat (1920)

Femme au chapeau
23 × 19½"　　Signed lower left
Mr. and Mrs. Lee A. Ault, New York
Exhibited:
1930 *Henri Matisse*, Galerie Thannhauser, Berl No. 45

1931 *Henri Matisse*, The Museum of Modern Art,
      New York. No. 45
1934 *French Painting from 15th Century to Present Day*,
      The California Palace of the Legion of Honor,
      San Francisco

*55 Interior at Nice   (1921)

Grand intérieur, Nice
52 × 35″   Signed lower right
The Art Institute of Chicago, gift of
Mrs. Gilbert W. Chapman
Exhibited:
1931 *Henri Matisse*, Galeries Georges Petit, Paris.
      No. 85
1933 *A Century of Progress*, The Art Institute of
      Chicago. No. 394
1948 *Henri Matisse Retrospective*, The Philadelphia
      Museum of Art. No. 54
1951-52 *Henri Matisse*, The Museum of Modern Art,
      New York; The Cleveland Museum of Art;
      The Art Institute of Chicago; The San
      Francisco Museum of Art. No. 53
1952 *Henri Matisse*, The Los Angeles Municipal Art
      Department, arranged by The Museum of
      Modern Art, New York. No. 36
1954 *Paintings by Henri Matisse*, Paul Rosenberg
      and Co., New York. No. 6
1955 *Six Centuries of Headdress*, Dallas Museum of
      Fine Arts, No. 21

*56 Moorish Screen   (1921-22)

Le paravent mauresque
36¼ × 29¼″   Signed lower right
The Philadelphia Museum of Art, bequest of
Lisa Norris Elkins
Exhibited:
1931 *Henri Matisse*, The Museum of Art, Rhode
      Island School of Design, Providence
1931 *Henri Matisse*, The Museum of Modern Art,
      New York. No. 59
1936 *Cent ans de théatre, musichall et cirque*, Galerie
      Bernheim-Jeune, Paris
1937 Fogg Art Museum, Harvard University,
      Cambridge
1939 *Sources of Modern Painting*, The Museum of Fine
      Arts, Boston. No. 51
1944-45 *French Paintings of the 20th Century*, Albright
      Art Gallery, Buffalo; Cincinnati Art Museum;
      The City Art Museum, St. Louis. No. 43
1947 *Masterpieces from Philadelphia Private Collections*,
      The Philadelphia Museum of Art. No. 73
1948 *Henri Matisse Retrospective*, The Philadelphia
      Museum of Art. No. 57
1952 University of Miami, Lowe Gallery.
1956 *Rétrospective Henri Matisse*, Musée National
      d'Art Moderne, Paris. No. 65

*57 Nude with Green Shawl   (1921-22)

Nu au châle vert
35 × 45¾″   Signed lower left
Lent anonymously
Exhibited:
1928 *XVIa Esposione Internazionale d'Arte della Città di
      Venezia* (as "*Odalisca su fondo rosso*"), Venice.
      No. 49
1954 *I "Fauves"*, XXVII Biennale di Venezia,
      Venice. No. 9

1955 *Rétrospective de Henri Matisse*, Salon d'Automne,
      Paris. No. 173
1960 *Matisse*, Pavillon de Vendôme, Aix-en-
      Provence. No. 18
1960 *Dix ans de la Biennale de Menton, les grands prix*,
      Musée Galliéra, Paris. No. 4

*58 Odalisque in Red Trousers   (1922)

L'odalisque à la culotte rouge
26⁵/₁₆ × 33¹/₁₆″   Signed lower right
Musée National d'Art Moderne, Paris
Exhibited:
1945-46 *Peintures du Musée d'Art Moderne* (circulating
      exhibition). No. 26
1948 *Art français*, Beirut, Lebanon
1951 *Henri Matisse*, National Museum of Tokyo.
1952 *La femme dans l'art*, Ostende.
1955 *La peinture française de l'impressionisme à nos jours*,
      Musée Municipal, Limoges.
1956 Akademie der Künste, Berlin
      Frankfurt and Luxembourg.
1963-64 *Exposition d'art français ancien et moderne*,
      Bombay, New Delhi, Calcutta,
      Madras and Hyderabad.
1964 *Figuration et défiguration: La figure humaine
      depuis Picasso*, Musée des Beaux-Arts, Ghent

*59 Checker Game and Piano Music   (1923)

Les joueurs de dames
29 × 36¼″   Signed lower right
Private Collection, New York
Exhibited:
1935 *12 Paintings by Six French Artists*, College Art
      Association, Durand-Ruel, Paris
1937 *Les Maîtres de l'art indépendant*, Musée d'Art
      Moderne de la Ville de Paris. No. 34
1946 *Les chefs-d'œuvre de collections privées françaises*,
      Musée de l'Orangerie, Paris

*60 Odalisque with Tambourine   (1923-24)

Odalisque au tambourin
36 × 25½″   Signed lower right
Lent anonymously
Exhibited:
1933-34 *Pittsburgh International*, Carnegie Institute,
      Pittsburgh; The Cleveland Museum of Art;
      The Toledo Museum of Art. No. 215
1937 *Les Maîtres de l'art indépendant*, Musée d'Art
      Moderne de la Ville de Paris

*61 Anemones   (1924)

Les anémones
28¾ × 36¼″   Signed lower left
Berner Kunstmuseum, Bern
Exhibited:
1947 Kunsthalle, Bern
1949 *Henri Matisse*, Musée des Beaux-Arts,
      Lucerne. No. 80
1950 *Henri Matisse*, Galerie des Ponchettes, Nice
1951 *Matisse*, Galerie M. Kaganovich, Paris
1953-54 Museum Boymans, Rotterdam
1959 Musée d'Art Moderne de la Ville de Paris
1961 *Franz. Malerei von Delacroix bis Picasso*,
      Volkswagenwerk, Wolfsburg

*62   Still Life in the Studio   (1924)

Nature morte dans l'atelier; L'intérieur à Nice
38½ × 31¼"   Signed lower right
Mrs. Albert D. Lasker, New York
Exhibited:
1951   *Impressionist Paintings*, M. Knoedler and Co.,
        Inc., New York
1952   *Contemporary Painting*, Dallas Museum
        of Fine Arts
1954   *Paintings from the Collection of Mrs. Albert
        D. Lasker*, California Palace of the Legion of
        Honor, San Francisco
1962   *Modern French Painting*, Wildenstein and Co.,
        New York; Rose Art Museum, Brandeis
        University, Waltham, Mass.

*63   Nude Seated on a Blue Cushion   (1924)

Nu au coussin bleu
28½ × 23"   Signed lower center
Mr. and Mrs. Sidney F. Brody, Los Angeles

*64   Reclining Nude, Back   (1927)

Nu étendu de dos
26 × 36¼"   Signed lower right
Private collection, Paris
Exhibited:
1931   *Henri Matisse*, The Museum of Modern Art,
        New York. No. 73
1931   *Henri Matisse*, Galerie Bernheim-Jeune, Paris
1946   *Matisse-Picasso*, Palais des Beaux-Arts,
        Universal and International Exhibition,
        Brussels. No. 8
1948   *Henri Matisse Retrospective*, The Philadelphia
        Museum of Art. No. 70
1949   *Henri Matisse*, Musée des Beaux-Arts, Lucerne.
        No. 86
1950   *Henri Matisse*, Galerie des Ponchettes, Nice
1956   *Rétrospective Henri Matisse*, Musée National
        d'Art Moderne, Paris. No. 75
1961   *Henri Matisse*, Musée Toulouse-Lautrec,
        Palais de la Berbie, Albi, France. No. 9

*65   Lemons on a Pewter Plate   (1927)

Citrons sur plat d'étain
21½ × 25¾"   Signed lower right
Mr. and Mrs. Nathan Cummings, Chicago
Exhibited:
1951-52   *Henri Matisse*, The Museum of Modern
        Art, New York; The Cleveland Museum of
        Art; The Art Institute of Chicago;
        The San Francisco Museum of Art. No. 60
1952   *Henri Matisse*, The Los Angeles Municipal
        Art Department, arranged by The Museum
        of Modern Art, New York. No. 38

66   Decorative Figure on an Ornamental
    Background   (1927)

Figure décorative sur fond ornemental
51³⁄₁₆ × 38½"   Signed lower left
Musée National d'Art Moderne, Paris
Exhibited:
1930   *Henri Matisse*, Galerie Thannhauser,
        Berlin. No. 73
1931   *Henri Matisse*, The Museum of Modern Art,
        New York. No. 70
1933   *Century of Progress - An Exhibition of Painting
        and Sculpture*, The Art Institute of Chicago.
        No. 39

1945   *Matisse-Picasso*, The Victoria and Albert
        Museum, London
1951-52   *Henri Matisse*, The Museum of Modern
        Art, New York; The Cleveland Museum o
        Art; The Art Institute of Chicago;
        The San Francisco Museum of Art. No. 59
1961-62   *Exposition d'art français contemporain*,
        National Museum of Modern Art, Tokyo;
        Kyoto National Museum

*67   Odalisque in an Armchair   1928

L'odalisque au fauteuil
23⅝ × 28¾"   Signed and dated lower left
Musée d'Art Moderne de la Ville de Paris
Exhibited:
1930   *Henri Matisse*, Galerie Thannhauser,
        Berlin. No. 76
1939   *Parijsche Schilders*, Amsterdam. No. 74
1939-40   *Pintura Francesa*, Buenos Aires. No. 181
1940   *The Painting of France Since the French
        Revolution*, The M. H. deYoung Memorial
        Museum, San Francisco. No. 147
1941   *From Cézanne to Picasso*, The Los Angeles
        County Museum of Art. No. 23
1941   *Masterpieces of French Painting*, The Portland
        Art Museum, Oregon
1949   *Henri Matisse*, Musée des Beaux-Arts,
        Lucerne. No. 89
1960   *Matisse*, Pavillon de Vendôme, Aix-en-
        Provence. No. 23

*68   Girl in a Yellow Dress   (1929-31)

Jeune fille en jaune
39⅜ × 32"   Signed lower left
The Baltimore Museum of Art, Cone Collection
Exhibited:
1933   *International*, Rockefeller Center, New York
        No. 81
1937   *Les Maîtres de l'art indépendant*,
        Musée d'Art Moderne de la Ville de Paris
1941   *A Century of Baltimore Collecting*, The
        Baltimore Museum of Art
1948   *Henri Matisse Retrospective*, The Philadelph
        Museum of Art. No. 75
1951-52   *Henri Matisse*, The Museum of Modern
        Art, New York; The Cleveland Museum
        of Art; The Art Institute of Chicago;
        The San Francisco Museum of Art. No. 6
1954   *Paintings by Matisse*, Paul Rosenberg and
        New York. No. 14
1955   *The Cone Collection*, M. Knoedler and Co.,
        Inc., New York

*69   Woman with a Turban   (1929-30)

Femme au turban
70⅞ × 59⅞"   Not signed
Private Collection, Paris

*70   Portrait of a Lady in White   (1933-34)

Portrait à la robe blanche
44½ × 28¾"   Not signed
Private Collection, Paris
Exhibited:
1960   *Matisse*, Pavillon de Vendôme, Aix-en-
        Provence. No. 24
1964   *Documenta III*, Kassel, Germany. p. 78

*71 Pink Nude 1935
Nu rose
26 × 36½″   Signed and dated lower left
The Baltimore Museum of Art, Cone Collection
Exhibited:
1953 *Trends and Origins of Contemporary Art*,
      The Denver Art Museum
1955 *The Cone Collection*, M. Knoedler and Co.,
      Inc., New York
1960 *Anatomy and Art*, William Rockhill Nelson
      Gallery of Art and Mary Atkins Museum of
      Fine Arts, Kansas City, Mo.
1961 *Franz. Malerei von Delacroix bis Picasso*,
      Volkswagenwerke, Wolfsburg

*72 The Dream 1935
Le rêve
31⅞ × 25⅝″   Signed and dated lower left
Mr. and Mrs. Pierre Matisse
Exhibited:
1936 *Henri Matisse*, Galerie Paul Rosenberg, Paris
1937 *Exposition des Maîtres de l'art indépendant*,
      Musée d'Art Moderne de la Ville de Paris
1949 *Henri Matisse*, Musée des Beaux-Arts,
      Lucerne. No. 91
1951-52 *Henri Matisse*, The Museum of Modern
      Art, New York; The Cleveland Museum
      of Art; The Art Institute of Chicago;
      The San Francisco Museum of Art. No. 64
1952 *Henri Matisse*, The Los Angeles Municipal
      Art Department, arranged by the Museum
      of Modern Art, New York. No. 40
1956 *Rétrospective Henri Matisse*, Musée National
      d'Art Moderne, Paris. No. 78

*73 Still Life with Three Vases 1935
Nature morte aux trois vases
28¾ × 23⅝″   Signed and dated lower right
Private Collection, Paris

*74 Nymph in the Forest (1936)
Nymphe dans la forêt
96 × 78″   Not signed
Private Collection, Paris

*75 Woman with Blue Jewel; Elena 1937
Femme au bijou bleu; Hélène
21½ × 13¼″   Signed and dated lower right
Mr. and Mrs. Taft Schreiber, Beverly Hills
Exhibited:
1938 *Recent Paintings by Matisse*, Galerie Paul
      Rosenberg, Paris
1954 *Paintings by Matisse*, Paul Rosenberg and Co.,
      New York. No. 16
1963 *The Bragaline Collection*, M. Knoedler and Co.,
      Inc., New York. No. 4

*76 Odalisque with Striped Robe 1937
Robe rayée, mauve et blanche
15 × 18″   Signed and dated upper right
Mr. and Mrs. Norton Simon, Los Angeles

*77 Lady in Blue 1937
Grande robe bleue, fond noir
36½ × 29″   Signed and dated lower left
Mrs. John Wintersteen, President, The Philadelphia
Museum of Art

Exhibited:
1947 *Masterpieces of Philadelphia Private Collections*,
      The Philadelphia Museum of Art. No. 92
1948 *Henri Matisse Retrospective*, The Philadelphia
      Museum of Art. No. 79
1954 *Paintings by Matisse*, Paul Rosenberg and Co.,
      New York. No. 15

*78 Odalisque in a Red Coat 1937
Odalisque au manteau rouge et tulipes violettes
21¼ × 18″   Signed and dated lower right
Private Collection, New York
Exhibited:
1937 *Matisse*, Galerie Paul Rosenberg, Paris. No. 19

*79 The Conservatory 1938
Le jardin d'hiver
28¼ × 23½″   Signed and dated lower right
Mr. and Mrs. Joseph Pulitzer, Jr., St. Louis
Exhibited:
1938 *Henri Matisse Paintings, Drawings of 1918
      to 1938*, Pierre Matisse Gallery, New York
1939 *Paintings by Henri Matisse*, Arts Club
      of Chicago
1941 *20th Century Art*, City Art Museum of
      St. Louis, Mo.
1951-52 *Henri Matisse*, The Museum of Modern
      Art, New York; The Cleveland Museum
      of Art; The Art Institute of Chicago;
      The San Francisco Museum of Art. No. 65
1954 *20th Century Art Loaned by the Members*,
      Arts Club of Chicago
1955 *The Arts of Matisse*, The Busch-Reisinger
      Museum, Cambridge.
1957 *Modern Painting, Drawing and Sculpture
      Collected by Louise and Joseph Pulitzer, Jr.*,
      M. Knoedler and Co., Inc.; Fogg Art Museum,
      Harvard University, Cambridge

*80 Pineapple and Anemones 1940
L'ananas et anémones
28½ × 35½″   Signed and dated lower right
Mrs. Albert D. Lasker, New York
Exhibited:
1951 *Impressionist Paintings*, M. Knoedler and Co.,
      Inc., New York
1953-54 *69 Paintings from the Collection of
      Mrs. Albert D. Lasker*
      Dallas Museum of Fine Arts, California
      Palace of the Legion of Honor, San Francisco
1955 *25th Anniversary Exhibition*, The Museum
      of Modern Art, New York
1957 *75th Birthday Anniversary*, League for
      Emotionally Disturbed Children,
      Paul Rosenberg and Co., New York
1960 *Summer Exhibition*, The Metropolitan Museum
      of Art, New York

*81 Sleeping Woman 1940
La dormeuse
31⅞ × 25½″   Signed and dated lower left
Private Collection, Paris
Exhibited:
1946 *Matisse-Picasso*, Palais des Beaux-Arts,
      Universal and International Exhibition,
      Brussels. No. 12

1948   *Henri Matisse Retrospective*, The Philadelphia Museum of Art. No. 82

1949   *Henri Matisse*, Musée des Beaux-Arts, Lucerne (as « Le rêve »). No. 102

1950   *XXV Biennale di Venezia*, Venice. No. 39

1960   *Matisse*, Pavillon de Vendôme, Aix-en-Provence (as « Le rêve »). No. 25

1964   *Documenta III*, Kassel, Germany. p. 78

*82   The Black Door   1942

La porte noire
24 × 15″   Signed and dated upper left
Heinz Berggruen, Paris

*83   Dancer and Armchair, Black Background   (1942)

Danseuse, fond noir, fauteuil rocaille; Danseuse au fauteuil rocaille
19¾ × 25⅝″   Signed lower right
Mrs. Marcel Duchamp, New York
Exhibited:

1949   *Henri Matisse*, Musée des BeauxArts, Lucerne. No. 108

1951-52   *Henri Matisse*, The Museum of Modern Art, New York; The Cleveland Museum of Art; The Art Institute of Chicago; The San Francisco Museum of Art. No. 68

1952   *Henri Matisse*, The Los Angeles Municipal Art Department, arranged by the Museum of Modern Art, New York. No. 43

*84   Lemons and Saxifrages   1943

Citrons et saxifrages
21¼ × 31⅞″   Signed and dated lower right
Siegfried Rosengart, Lucerne
Exhibited:

1949   *Henri Matisse*, Musée des Beaux-Arts, Lucerne. No. 110

1961   *Da Boldini a Pollak*, Torino. No. 114

1964   *Chefs-d'œuvre des collections suisses de Manet à Picasso*, Exposition National Suisse, Palais de Beaulieu, Lausanne. No. 291

*85   The Lute   1943

Le luth
23⅜ × 31⅜″   Signed and dated lower left
Mr. and Mrs. Sidney F. Brody, Los Angeles

*86   Tabac Royal; Michaella; Interior at Nice   1943

Intérieur à Nice
25 × 31½″   Signed and dated upper right
Mrs. Albert D. Lasker, New York
Exhibited:

1951   *Impressionist Paintings*, M. Knoedler and Co., Inc., New York

1953-54   *69 Paintings from the Collection of Mrs. Albert D. Lasker* Dallas Museum of Fine Arts; The California Palace of the Legion of Honor San Francisco

1956   *Rétrospective Henri Matisse*, Musée National d'Art Moderne, Paris. No. 89

1958   Musée des Beaux-Arts, Liège, Belgium

1960   *Summer Exhibition*, The Metropolitan Museum of Art, New York

*87   The Silence Living in Houses   1947

Le silence habité des maisons
21⅝ × 18⅛″   Signed and dated lower left
Private Collection, Paris
Exhibited:

1947   Salon d'Automne, Paris

1949   *Henri Matisse œuvres récentes*, Musée National d'Art Moderne, Paris. No. 3

1950   *XXV Biennale di Venezia*, Venice. No. 43

1950   *Henri Matisse*, Galerie des Ponchettes, Nice

1955   *Rétrospective Henri Matisse*, Salon d'Automne, Paris

1956   *Rétrospective Henri Matisse*, Musée National d'Art Moderne, Paris. No. 93

1961   *Henri Matisse*, Musée Toulouse-Lautrec, Palais de la Berbie, Albi. No. 14

*88   Interior with Figure   1947

Figure dans un intérieur
36¼ × 28¾″   Signed and dated lower right
Private Collection, Paris

*89   The Pineapple   1948

L'ananas
45¾ × 35″   Signed and dated lower right
The Alex Hillman Corporation, New York
Exhibited:

1949   *Henri Matisse œuvres récentes*, Musée National d'Art Moderne, Paris. No. 9

1951-52   *Henri Matisse*, The Museum of Modern Art New York; The Cleveland Museum of Art; The Art Institute of Chicago; The San Francisco Museum of Art. No. 71

1956   *Rétrospective Henri Matisse*, Musée National d'Art Moderne, Paris. No. 94

*90   Large Interior in Red   1948

Grand intérieur rouge
57½ × 38¼″   Signed and dated lower left
Musée National d'Art Moderne, Paris
Exhibited:

1949   *Henri Matisse œuvres récentes*, Musée National d'Art Moderne, Paris. No. 13

1950   *XXV Biennale di Venezia*, Venice. No. 45

1950-51   *L'Ecole de Paris 1900-1950*, Royal Academy Burlington House, London. No. 43

1951-52   *Henri Matisse*, The Museum of Modern Art, New York; The Cleveland Museum of Art; The Art Institute of Chicago; The San Francisco Museum of Art. No. 72

1956   *Dix ans de peinture française*, Musée des Beaux-Arts, Grenoble.

*91   Interior with Black Fern   1948

Intérieur à la fougère noire
45⁹⁄₁₆ × 35″   Signed and dated lower center
Mr. and Mrs. Otto Preminger, New York
Exhibited:

1949   *Henri Matisse œuvres récentes*, Musée National d'Art Moderne. No. 12

*92   Woman in a Blue Gandoura Robe   1951

Portrait à la gandoura bleue
32 × 25½″   Signed and dated lower right
Jean Matisse, Paris
Exhibited:

1961   *Henri Matisse*, Musée Toulouse-Lautrec, Palais de la Berbie, Albi, France. No. 16

SCULPTURE

*93a   Profile of a Woman, Medaillon   1894
Profil de Femme
M 180 bis   2/3   Diameter 10″
Private Collection, Paris

*93   Jaguar Devouring a Hare—after Barye   (1899-1901)
Jaguar dévorant un lièvre   d'après Barye
M 144   9/10   9″
Pierre Matisse

*94   Old Woman, Bust   (1900)
Buste ancien; Buste de femme
M 155   2/10   24½″
The Joseph H. Hirshhorn Collection, New York

*95   Study of a Foot   (1900)
Etude de pied
M 152   4/10   12″
Charles E. Slatkin Galleries, New York

*96   The Slave   (1900-03)
Le serf
M 121   7/10   36¼″
The Joseph H. Hirshhorn Collection, New York

*97   Madeleine I (round base)   (1901)
M 123   4/10   23⅝″
Charles E. Slatkin Galleries, New York

*98   Madeleine II (square base)   (1903)
M 153   9/10   23⅝″
Private Collection, Paris

*99   Woman Leaning on her Hands   (1905)
Femme appuyée sur les mains
M 124   5¼″
Mr. and Mrs. Norton Simon, Los Angeles

*100   Child's Head (Pierre)   (1905)
Tête d'enfant (Pierre)
M 138   8/10   6⅜″
Private Collection, New York

*101   Head of a Faun   (1905)
Tête de faune
M 166   2/10   6¼″
Jean Matisse, Paris

*102   Head of a Young Girl (Marguerite)   (1906)
Tête de fillette (Marguerite)
M 126   9/10   6½″
Frank Perls, Beverly Hills

*103   Nude Braced, Arms on Head   (1906)
Nu campé, bras sur la tête; Nu debout, bras levés
M 132   10/10   10″
Mrs. Bertram Smith, New York

*104   Standing Nude   (1906)
Nu de fillette; Nu debout
M 139   3/10   19″
Private Collection, Paris

Dimensions refer to height; all sculptures listed are cast in bronze.

The numbers preceded by the letter M (Matisse) refer to a Matisse family list of bronzes of all the artist's sculpture, which will eventually be published.

An M number has been given each sculpture on the date of casting. However, the date of the sculpture refers to the date of the completion of the original.

All bronzes of Henri Matisse consist of editions of 10, with the exceptions of no. 93a (edition of 3) and no. 134 (edition of 5)

*105 Reclining Figure in a Chemise (1906)
Nu couché à la chemise
M 127 6″
The Joseph H. Hirshhorn Collection, New York

*106 Small Head with Flat Nose (1906)
Petite tête au nez camus; Tête de fillette, Marguerite
M 167 6/10 5½″
The Joseph H. Hirshhorn Collection, New York

*107 Small Head with Pompadour (1907)
Petite tête aux cheveux striés; Tête de fillette avec coiffure relevée devant
M 170 10/10 4⅝″
Jean Matisse, Paris

*108 Girl's Head with Necklace (1907)
Tête au collier; Tête de fillette au collier
M 130 7/10 6⅛″
Mrs. Charles Payson, Manhasset, Long Island

*109 Reclining Nude I, Collioure (1907)
Nu couché I
M 129 6/10 13⅞″
The Baltimore Museum of Art, Cone Collection

*110 Decorative Figure (1908)
Figure décorative
M 169 4/10 29″
The Joseph H. Hirshhorn Collection, New York

*111 Two Negresses (1908)
Deux négresses
M 122 1/10 18½″
The Joseph H. Hirshhorn Collection, New York

*112 Standing Torso, without Arms or Head (1909)
Torse debout, sans bras ni tête; Torse sans bras, ni tête
M 160 5/10 9¾″
The Joseph H. Hirshhorn Collection, New York

*113 The Serpentine (1909)
La serpentine
M 142 10/10 22¼″
Pierre Matisse

*114 Seated Nude, Arm Behind Back (1909)
Nu assis, bras derrière le dos
M 131 9/10 11½″
Private Collection, Paris

*115 Seated Nude (Olga) (1910)
Nu assis
M 143 0/10 16½″
Jean Matisse, Paris

*116 Head of Jeanette I (1910-13)
Tête de Jeanette I
M 150 7/10 12½″
The Joseph H. Hirshhorn Collection, New York

*117 Head of Jeanette II (1910-13)
Tête de Jeanette II
M 149 7/10 10½″
The Joseph H. Hirshhorn Collection, New York

*118 Head of Jeanette III (1910-13)
Tête de Jeanette III
M 148 2/10 24″
Mr. and Mrs. Norton Simon, Los Angeles

*119 Head of Jeanette IV (1910-13)
Tête de Jeanette IV
M 151 3/10 24½″
The Joseph H. Hirshhorn Collection, New York

*120 Head of Jeanette V (1910-13)
Tête de Jeanette V
M 168 1/10 22⅞″
Jean Matisse, Paris

*121 The Dance (1911)
La danse
M 176 1/10 16⅛″
The Joseph H. Hirshhorn Collection, New York

*122 Head of Marguerite (1915)
Tête de Marguerite
M 125 3/10 12⅝″
Pierre Matisse

*123 Crouching Nude, Arms Around the Right Leg (1918)
Nu accroupi, bras autour de la jambe droite; Figure accroupie
M 157 9/10 9″
Paul Rosenberg and Co., New York

*124 Crouching Venus (1918)
Vénus accroupie
M 156 4/10 10¼″
Private Collection, New York

*125 Large Seated Nude (1922-25)
Grand nu assis
M 159 2/10 30¾″
The Minneapolis Institute of Arts

*126 Small Nude in an Armchair (1924)
Petit nu au canapé; Nu au canapé
M 184 0/10 9⅜″
Pierre Matisse

*127   Henriette, Second State   (1927)
Henriette, deuxième état; Grosse Tête (Henriette)
M 140   6/10   12⅝"
The San Francisco Museum of Art,
Harriet Lane Levy Bequest

*128   Reclining Nude II   (1927-29)
Nu couché II
M 179   5/10   11"
Mr. and Mrs. Sidney F. Brody, Los Angeles

*129   Henriette, Third State (1929)
Head of Henriette (Stout Head)
*Tête souriante, Henriette, troisième état; Grosse tête
(Henriette)*
M 163   5/10   15¾"
Private Collection, Paris

*130   Reclining Nude III   (1929)
Nu couché III (torse ronde)
M 154   9/10   7½"
Charles E. Slatkin Galleries, New York

*131   Venus in a Shell   (1930)
Venus à la coquille
M 173   0/10   12½"
Pierre Matisse

*132   Tiari (with necklace)   (1930)
Le tiaré (au collier)
M 175   1/10   8⅛"
The Baltimore Museum of Art, Cone Collection

*133   Venus in a Shell   (1932)
Venus à la coquille
M 183   3/10   13½"
The Joseph H. Hirshhorn Collection, New York

*134   Christ, Vence Chapel   (1950)
Christ, Chapelle de Vence
M 189   0/1   13¾"
Jean Matisse, Paris

*135   Bas Relief I (1909)
M 146   6/10   74⅜×44½"
Lent anonymously

*136   Bas Relief II   (1913)
M 181   6/10   74¼×44⅝"
Lent anonymously

*137   Bas Relief III   (1916-17)
M 145   6/10   74½×44¾"
Lent anonymously

*138   Bas Relief IV   (1930)
M 147   6/10   74×44½   "
Lent anonymously

DRAWINGS

*139 Seated Model, Hands Clasping Knee; Nude Study
(1900)

Figure assise
Pencil 13¹/₁₆ ×8⁹/₁₆″ Signed lower right
The Metropolitan Museum of Art, gift of
Mrs. Florence Blumenthal 1910

140 Woman Leaning on Her Hands (1905)

Femme appuyée sur les mains
Pen and ink 6¾ ×8¾″
Private Collection, Paris

*141 Head of Marguerite Reading (1905)

La liseuse (tête de Marguerite)
Pen and ink 15⅝ ×20½″ Signed lower rig
The Museum of Modern Art, New York,
acquired through the Lillie P. Bliss Bequest

*142 Nude in a Chair (1905)

Nu endormi dans une chaise
Brush with India ink 25⅞ ×18⅜″
Signed lower right
The Art Institute of Chicago, gift of
Mrs. Potter Palmer

*143 Nude with Pipes (Study for *Joy of Life*) (1906)

Etude pour Joie de vivre
Pen and ink 18 ×23¾″
Signed lower right
Mr. and Mrs. Richard S. Davis, London

144 Standing Nude (1906-07)

Nu debout
Pencil 12⅞ ×8½″ Signed lower right
The Art Institute of Chicago,
gift of Emily Crane Chadbourne

145 Nude Study, Back (1906-07)

Nu, étude
Pencil 11¹⁵/₁₆ ×8¹⁵/₁₆″ Signed lower right
The Metropolitan Museum of Art, New York,
gift of Mrs. Florence Blumenthal 1910

146 Nude Resting Knee on Chair (1906-07)

Nu, genou sur une chaise
Pencil 12⅜ ×9½″ Signed lower right
The Art Institute of Chicago,
The Alfred Stieglitz Collection

147 Figure Study (1907)

Figure, étude
Pen and ink 10⅜ ×8″ Signed lower right
The Museum of Modern Art, New York,
gift of Edward Steichen

148   Two Girl Musicians   (1921)

Les deux musiciennes
Pencil   14⅜ ×9⅝″   Signed lower right
The Fogg Art Museum, Harvard University,
Cambridge, Meta and Paul J. Sachs Bequest

149   Standing Nude   (1908)

Nu debout
(probably study for the *Bathers with a Turtle*, No. 26)
Black crayon   12¼ ×9¼″   Signed lower right
The Art Institute of Chicago,
The Alfred Stieglitz Collection

150   Standing Nude, Study   (1908)

Nu, étude
Pencil   12¹/₁₆ ×9³/₁₆″   Signed lower right
The Metropolitan Museum of Art,
gift of Mrs. Florence Blumenthal   1910

*151   The Dance   (1909-10)

La danse
Pen and ink   6½ ×9″
Private Collection, Paris

*152   The Dance   (1909-10)

La danse
Ink India   11 ×9″   Signed lower right
Private Collection, Paris

*153   Seated Woman Clasping Her Right Knee;
Woman Nursing Knee; a Foot   (1909)

Nu assis
(Study for the piper in *Music*, Moscow)
Reed pen and ink   11⅝ ×9¼″
Signed and dated lower right
The Art Institute of Chicago,
gift of Emily Crane Chadbourne

*154   Young Girl with Tulips   (1910)

Jeune fille aux tulipes
(Study for *Young Girl with Tulips*, Leningrad)
Charcoal   30×24″
Private Collection, Paris

*155   Study for Painting of Marguerite Matisse of 1910

Etude pour Jeune fille au chat noir
(Study for Girl with Black Cat, No. 30)
Pencil   10¾ ×8¼″   Signed lower right
The Art Institute fo Chicago,
gift of Emily Crane Chadbourne

*156   Jean and Pierre Matisse Playing Checkers   1911

Les joueurs de dames
Black crayon   19 ×24¾″
Signed and dated lower right
Private Collection, Paris

*157   Portrait of Sergei I. Shchukin   (1912)

Portrait de Serge I. Stchoukine
Charcoal   19½ ×12″   Signed lower right
Pierre Matisse

*158   Portrait of Mrs. S. D. Warren, née Mabel Bayard
(1913)
Pencil   11⅛ ×8½″   Signed lower right
The Museum of Fine Arts, Boston,
gift of Mrs. J. Gardner Bradley, Mrs. Warren Thayer
and Miss Sylvia Warren

*159   Portrait of Miss Harriet Lane Levy   1913
Pencil   10⅞ ×8⅜″   Signed and dated lower left
The San Francisco Museum of Art,
Harriet Lane Levy Bequest

*160   Elsa Glaser   (1914)
Pencil   11¼ ×9″   Signed and dated lower left
The Art Institute of Chicago, gift of
Mrs. Margaret Blake

*161   Greta Prozor   (1916)
Charcoal   22½ ×15″   Signed lower left
Private Collection, Paris

162   Seated Nude   (1917)

Nu assis
Pencil   15⅜ ×11⅜″   Signed lower right
The Museum of Modern Art, New York,
gift of Abby Aldrich Rockefeller

*163   Antoinette Wearing Plumed Hat   (1919)

Antoinette au chapeau à plumes
Pen and ink   11 ×14″   Signed lower right
The Art Institute of Chicago,
gift of The Arts Club of Chicago

*164   The Plumed Hat   1919

Le chapeau à plumes
Pencil   13¾ ×11½″
Signed and dated lower left
Mrs. Hildegard Ault Tjeder, New York

*165   The Plumed Hat   1919
Le chapeau à plumes
Pencil   20⅞ × 14⅜″
Signed and dated lower left
The Detroit Institute of Arts,
bequest of John S. Newberry

*166   Seated Nude with Arms Raised;
Nude in an Armchair   (1920)
Nu assis aux bras levés
Charcoal   24 × 19½″
Signed lower right
The Art Institute of Chicago,
The Wirt D. Walker Fund

167   Study for Odalisque with Magnolias   (1924)
Etude pour Odalisque aux magnolias
Charcoal   16 × 20¼″   Signed lower right
The Museum of Modern Art, New York,
Katherine S. Dreier Bequest

*168   Nude with Raised Arms   (1923)
Nu aux bras levés
Charcoal   12⅜ × 18⅞″   Signed lower right
Mr. and Mrs. James E. Pollak, Los Angeles

*169   Standing Nude with Raised Arms   (1922-23)
Nu debout aux bras levés
Charcoal   20 × 15″   Signed lower left
Heinz Berggruen, Paris

170   Nude, Back   (1927)
Nu de dos
Charcoal   12 × 9¼″
Private Collection, Paris

*171   Nude, Back   (1927)
Nu de dos
(Study for Reclining Nude, Back, No. 64)
Pencil   11 × 14½″   Signed lower right
Private Collection, Paris

*172   Study for Decorative Figure   1927
Etude pour figure décorative
(Study for Decorative Figure on an Ornamental
Background, No. 66)
Charcoal   24¾ × 19″   Signed and dated
lower left
Private Collection, Paris

173   Two Reclining Figures   1928
Deux figures couchées
Pen and ink   12½ × 20″
Signed and dated lower right
Private Collection, Paris

*174   Standing Odalisque, Veiled   1930
Odalisque debout voilée
Pencil   12 × 9¼″   Signed and dated lower rig
Frank Perls, Beverly Hills

175   Portrait of John Dewey   1930
Charcoal   24⅜ × 19″
Signed and dated lower right
The Museum of Modern Art, New York,
gift of Pierre Matisse

*176   Portrait of Dr. Claribel Cone   (1934)
Charcoal   23¼ × 16″   Signed lower right
The Baltimore Museum of Art, Cone Collection

177   Faun and Nymph   (1935)
Faune et nymphe
(Study for illustration of *Ulysses* by James Joyce)
Charcoal   22 × 25″   Signed lower left
Private Collection, Paris

*178   Nude in the studio; Reclining Nude   1935
Nu dans l'atelier
Pen and ink   17¾ × 22⅜″
Signed and dated lower right
Private Collection, New York

*179   Nude Seated on a Stool   1936
Nu au tabouret
Charcoal   20⅝ × 16″
Signed and dated lower right
Private Collection, Zurich

180   Landscape   (1936)
Paysage
Pencil   10¾ × 8¼″
Private Collection, Paris

*181   Self Portrait   1937
Auto-portrait
Charcoal   10⅛ × 10″
Signed and dated lower right
Private Collection, Paris

182   Artist and Model Reflected in a Mirror   1937
L'artiste et son modèle reflétés dans la glace
Pen and black ink   24 × 16″
Signed and dated lower right
The Baltimore Museum of Art, Cone Collection

*183   The Rumanian Blouse   (1937)
La blouse roumaine
Pen and black ink   25 × 19½″
Signed lower left
The Baltimore Museum of Art, Cone Collection

*184　Head of a Woman, I　1937
Tête de femme, I
Ink　24 × 16⅛″　Signed and dated lower right
Santa Barbara Museum of Art,
gift of Wright Saltus Ludington

185　Head of a Woman, II　1937
Tête de femme, II
Ink　24¹/₁₆ × 16³/₁₆″　Signed and dated lower left
Santa Barbara Museum of Art,
gift of Wright Saltus Ludington

186　Portrait of Professor Whittemore　1937
Charcoal　20½ × 16″
Signed and dated lower left
Private Collection, Paris

187　Back of a Reclining Nude　1938
Nu couché de dos
Charcoal　24¼ × 32½″
Signed and dated lower left
Private Collection, Paris

*188　Two Women　1938
Deux figures de femmes
Pen and ink　15 × 20¼″
Signed and dated lower right
Private Collection, Paris

*189　Seated Woman　1938
Femme assise
Charcoal　19¼ × 15″
Signed and dated lower right
Galerie Beyeler, Basel

*190　Sleeping Girl　1939
La dormeuse
(Study for Sleeping Woman, No. 81)
Pencil　21 × 16″　Signed and dated lower right
Private Collection, Paris

*191　Asiatic Lady　1939
L'Asiatique
Charcoal　23⅛ × 15¼″
Signed and dated lower right
Dr. and Mrs. Franklin D. Murphy, Los Angeles

*192　Mother Nursing Child　1939
Maternité
Charcoal　25½ × 19¾″
Signed and dated lower right
The Joseph H. Hirshhorn Collection, New York

193　Young Woman and Still Life　1939
Jeune femme et nature morte
Ink　29 × 39″　Signed and dated lower right
University of California, Los Angeles,
Grunwald Graphic Arts Foundation,
gift of Dr. and Mrs. McKinley Helm

194　Self Portrait　1941
Auto-portrait
Sanguine　19 × 14¾″
Signed and dated lower right
Pierre Matisse

*195　Theme A, Variation 2　1941
Thèmes et variations, A 2
Pen and ink　24¾ × 19⅝″
Signed and dated lower right
P. N. Matisse Gallery, Beverly Hills

*196　Theme A, Variations 5　1941
Thèmes et variations, A 5
Pen and ink　21⅛ × 16″
Signed and dated lower right
Private Collection, Paris

*197　Theme E, Variation 9　1941
Thèmes et variations, E 9
Pen and ink　21⅛ × 16″
Signed and dated lower right
Private Collection, Paris

*198　Theme F, Variation 1　1941
Thèmes et variations, F 1
Charcoal　15¾ × 20½″
Signed and dated lower right
Grenoble, Musée de Peinture et de Sculpture

*199　Theme F, Variation 3　1941
Thèmes et variations, F 3
Pen and ink　20½ × 15¾″
Signed and dated lower right
Grenoble, Musée de Peinture et de Sculpture

200　Theme H, Variation 8　1941
Thèmes et variations, H 8
Pen and ink　15¾ × 20½″
Signed and dated lower right
Grenoble, Musée de Peinture et de Sculpture

*201　Theme L, Variation 2　1942
Thèmes et variations, L 2
Lithographic crayon　13 × 20½″
Signed and dated lower right
Pierre Matisse

202   Theme L, Variation 16   1942
Thèmes et variations, L16
Lithographic crayon   20⅝×16″
Signed and dated lower left
Pierre Matisse

203   Theme N, Variation 1   1942
Thèmes et variations, N1
Charcoal   21×18¼″
Signed and dated lower right
Private Collection, Paris

204   Theme N, Variation 6   1942
Thèmes et variations, N6
Pen and ink   20¾×16″
Signed and dated lower right
Pierre Matisse

205   Theme N, Variation 7   1942
Thèmes et variations, N7
Pen and ink   21¼×16″
Signed and dated lower left
Private Collection, Paris

206   Theme O, Variation 4   1942
Thèmes et variations, O4
Pencil   21×16″
Signed and dated lower left
Private Collection, Paris

*207   Branch of a Judas Tree   1942
Branche d'arbre de Judas
Charcoal   10×15½″   Inscribed lower right
"à John Rewald. Henri Matisse 8/42"
Mr. and Mrs. John Rewald, New York

208   Fragrance   1942
Les arômes
Pen and ink   21×16″
Signed and dated upper left
Pierre Matisse

209   Fragrance   (1943)
Les arômes
Charcoal   30×22¼″   Signed lower left
Pierre Matisse

*210   Haiti   (1943)
Pen and ink   20½×15½″   Signed lower right
Mr. and Mrs. Ray Stark, Los Angeles

*211   Interior   1944
Intérieur
Charcoal   15½×20½″
Signed and dated lower left
The Joseph H. Hirshorn Collection, New York

*212   Table Still Life   1945
Nature morte sur une table
Pen and ink   15½×20½″
Signed and dated lower left
Dr. and Mrs. David I. Elterman, Sherman Oaks,
California

213   Woman at a Table   1944
Femme à la table
Pen and ink   20¾×16″
Signed and dated lower left
Mr. and Mrs. Sidney F. Brody, Los Angeles

214   Self Portrait   (1945)
Auto-portrait
Crayon   16⅛×20⅜″   Signed lower left
The Museum of Modern Art, New York,
John S. Newberry Fund

215   Head of a Girl   (1947)
Tête de jeune fille
Chinese ink   13×10″   Signed lower right
Private Collection, Paris

*216   Dahlias and Pomegranates   1947
Dahlias et grenades
Brush and ink   30⅛×22¼″
Signed and dated lower left
The Museum of Modern Art, New York,
Abby Aldrich Rockefeller Fund

*217   Interior   1948
Intérieur
Chinese ink   35×23″
Signed and dated lower right
Private Collection, Paris

218   Study for "Christ Before Pilate,"
for Stations of the Cross   (1949)
Etude pour "Le Christ devant Pilate," Chemin de Croix
Chinese ink with brush   26×20″
Signed lower right
Musée Matisse, Cimiez-Nice

*219   Study for "Christ Before Pilate,"
for Stations of the Cross   (1949)
Etude pour "Le Christ devant Pilate, Chemin de Croix"
Chinese ink with brush   26×20″
Signed lower right
Musée Matisse, Cimiez-Nice

*220   Large Head of a Woman   (1952)
Grande tête de femme
Chinese ink   25⅞×19⅞″   Signed lower left
Mrs. Vicci Sperry, Los Angeles

221   Large Head of a Woman   (1950)
Grande tête de femme
Chinese ink   25⅞×19⅞″   Signed lower left
Mrs. Vicci Sperry, Los Angeles

GRAPHICS

Graphic dimensions refer to the size of the plate and do not include the margins unless otherwise indicated.

The designation of plate numbers has been established by the Matisse family as a means of cataloguing the graphic works of Matisse.

These plate references have been carefully checked with the family for this listing to conform with their records. Plate numbers are chronological by date of printing. These dates do not always correspond with the date of the artist's original work.

Wherever possible, reproduction references from the following books are indicated below, for those graphics not herein reproduced:

B. Alfred H. Barr. Jr. *Matisse: His Art and His Public* (New York: The Museum of Modern Art, 1951)

Berg 1952 Berggruen & Cie. *Henri Matisse, gravures récentes* (Paris: Berggruen, 1952)

Berg 1954 Berggruen & Cie. *Henri Matisse, lighographies rares* (Paris: Berggruen, 1954)

L. William S. Lieberman. *Matisse, 50 Years of His Graphic Art* (New York: George Braziller, Inc., 1956)

L.E. William S. Lieberman. *Etchings by Matisse* (New York: The Museum of Modern Art, 1955)

*222 Sketches: Nudes and Children's Heads, Jean and Marguerite (Second state) (1900-1901)
Esquisses: nus et têtes d'enfants, Jean et Marguerite (deuxième état)
Drypoint Pl. 55 *Etat* 5^{13}/$_{16}$×4″
Jean Matisse, Paris

*223 Studies of a Woman in Street Costume (1900-01)
Deux études d'une femme en costume
Drypoint Pl. 56 *Etat* 5¼×3½″
Jean Matisse, Paris

*224 Three Studies of a Nude (1900-01)
Nu, trois études
Drypoint Pl. 57 8/8 5×3½″
The Art Institute of Chicago, gift of Mr. and Mrs. Carl Schniewind

*225 Self Portrait as an Etcher (1903)
Le graveur, auto-portrait
Etching with drypoint Pl. 52 20/30 5⅞×7⅞″
The Metropolitan Museum of Art, New York, Dick Fund

226 Sketches: Nudes (First state) (c.1903)
Esquisses: nus (premier état)
Drypoint Pl. 55 *Etat* 5^{13}/$_{16}$×4″
The Museum of Modern Art, New York
Reproduced: L.*p.34 (left)*

227 Nude (c.1903)
Nu
Drypoint Pl. 56 bis 3/30 5⅞×3^{13}/$_{16}$″
The Museum of Modern Art, New York
Reproduced: L.*p.35 (left)*

*228 Nude (1904)
Nu
Lithograph Pl. 29 38/50 11^{3}/$_{16}$×9^{15}/$_{16}$″
(including margins)
Jean Matisse, Paris

229 Head of Woman with Eyes Closed (1906)
Tête de femme, les yeux fermés
Lithograph Pl. 1 22/25 17½×11″
The Art Institute of Chicago,
The Alfred Stieglitz Collection
Reproduced: L. *p.85*
(Shown Art Institute of Chicago only)

230 Standing Nude with Arms Folded (1906)
Nu debout aux bras croisés
Lithograph Pl. 2 2/25 17×9^{11}/$_{16}$″
The Museum of Modern Art, New York, gift of Victor S. Riesenfeld
Reproduced: L. *p.89*

*231 Standing Nude with Downcast Eyes (1906)
Idole
Lithograph Pl. 2 bis 12/25 17½×8½″
The Art Institute of Chicago,
The Alfred Stieglitz Collection
(Shown Art Institute of Chicago only)

*232 Upturned Head (1906)
Tête renversée
Lithograph Pl. 5 10/25 11⅛×10¾″
The Museum of Modern Art, New York, gift of Abby Aldrich Rockefeller

233 Nude (1906)
Nu
Lithograph Pl. 10 bis   17/25   17¹/₁₆ × 10⅛"
(including margins)
Jean Matisse, Paris
Reproduced: L. *p.93*

*234 Nude, The Large Woodcut   (1906)
Nu, le grand bois
Woodcut   33/50   18¾ × 15"
The Museum of Modern Art, New York, gift of
Mr. and Mrs. R. Kirk Askew, Jr.

*235 Woodblock for: Nude, The Large Woodcut   (1906)
Bois pour: Nu, le grand bois
Woodblock   19½ × 15¾"
Frank Perls, Beverly Hills

*236 Nude, The Light Woodcut   (1906)
Nu, le bois clair
Woodcut   41/50   13½ × 10"
University of California, Los Angeles,
Norton Simon Collection

237 Nude, The Dark Woodcut   (1906)
Nu, le bois foncé
Woodcut   45/50   12¼ × 8½"
University of California, Los Angeles,
Norton Simon Collection
Reproduced: L. *p.65*

*238 Torso, Face Partly Showing; Nude with Face Half
Hidden   (1912)
Torse au visage coupé
Lithograph Pl. 15   16/50   19¾ × 12"
The Art Institute of Chicago,
The Alfred Stieglitz Collection

239 Woman in Kimono (Madame Matisse)   (1914)
Femme en kimono
Drypoint Pl. 12   8/15   6³/₁₆ × 2⅜"
The Brooklyn Museum, gift of
Louis E. Stern Foundation

240 Seated Nude   (1914)
Nu assis
Drypoint Pl. 48   3/12   5½ × 3½"
Jean Matisse, Paris
Reproduced: L.E. *p.12*

241 Joan Massia   (1914)
Etching Pl. 9   3/15   9⅝ × 7⅝"
The Museum of Modern Art, New York,
Larry Aldrich Fund
Reproduced: L. p. 37 (right)

242 Mademoiselle Yvonne Landsberg   (1914)
Etching Pl. 17   20/30   6¼ × 2⅜"
The Metropolitan Museum of Art, New York,
Dick Fund
Reproduced: L. p. 38 (left)

243 Madame Demetrius Galanis   (1914)
Etching Pl. 20   7/15   6³/₁₆ × 2⅜"
The Metropolitan Museum of Art, New York,
Dick Fund
Reproduced: L. *p. 46* (right)

244 Emma La Forge   (1914)
Etching Pl. 21   3/5   3½ × 2⁵/₁₆"
The Metropolitan Museum of Art, New York
Reproduced: L. *p. 42* (right)

245 Portrait of Bourgeat   (1914)
Etching Pl. 23   11/15   7 × 5"
The Brooklyn Museum
Reproduced: L. *p.36*; L.E. *p.5*

246 Profile of Madame Derain   (1914)
Etching Pl. 25   10/15   3⅝ × 2½"
The Art Institute of Chicago, given by Mrs. Gilbert
W. Chapman in memory of Charles B. Goodspeed

247 Walter Pach   (1914)
Etching Pl. 33   9/15   6⅛ × 2¼"
Jean Matisse, Paris
Reproduced: L. *p.47*; B. *p.398*

248 Olivares   (1914)
Etching Pl. 34   2/15   7½ × 5¹/₁₆"
The Metropolitan Museum of Art, New York,
Dick Fund
Reproduced: L. *p.47 (left)*

249 Matthew Stewart Prichard   (1914)
Etching Pl. 38   *Essai*   7¾ × 6"
Jean Matisse, Paris
Reproduced: L. *p.41*

*250 Loulou in a Flowered Hat   (1914)
Loulou au chapeau à fleurs
Etching Pl. 41   14/15   7¹/₁₆ × 5"
The Museum of Modern Art, New York

251 Margot in a Japanese Robe   (1914)
Margot en robe Japonaise
Etching Pl. 43   8/10   7¹¹/₁₆ × 4¼"
The Museum of Modern Art, New York

252 Three Studies of a Nude (1914)
Nu: trois études
Etching and drypoint Pl. 50   Proof   5⅞ × 3⅞"
The Museum of Modern Art, New York
Reproduced: L.E. *p.15*; B. *p. 398*

253 Black Eyes   (1914)
Les yeux noirs
Lithograph Pl. 18   44/50   17⅞ × 12¾"
Private Collection, Paris
Reproduced: L. *p.97*

*254 Seated Nude, Back Turned   (1914)
Nu assis, vu de dos
Lithograph Pl. 19   16⁹/₁₆ × 10⅜"
The Metropolitan Museum of Art, New York,
Rogers Fund

*255 Double Portrait of Josette Gris   (1916)
Etching Pl. 32   9/15   5¹/₁₆×7⅛″
The Metropolitan Museum of Art, New York,
Dick Fund

256 Apples   (1916-17)
Pommes
Monotype Pl. 19   2¼ ×6⅛″
The Museum of Modern Art, New York,
Abby Aldrich Rockefeller Fund
Reproduced: L. p.72 (top)

*257 Torso   (1916-17)
Torse
Monotype Pl. 13   6¹⁵/₁₆ ×5¹/₁₆″
The Museum of Modern Art, New York

*258 Seated Nude with Arms Crossed   (1916-17)
Nu assis, bras croisés
Monotype   7 × 5¹/₁₆″
The Metropolitan Museum of Art, New York,
gift of Stephan Bourgeois

*259 Interior, Artist Drawing Three Apples   (1916-17)
Intérieur, l'artiste dessine des pommes
Monotype   3¹³/₁₆ ×5⅞″
The Museum of Modern Art, New York, gift of
Abby Aldrich Rockefeller

260 Greta Prozor   (1916)
Drypoint Pl. 105   11/15   5¹⁵/₁₆ ×4⁵/₁₆″
University of California, Los Angeles,
Grunwald Graphic Arts Foundation

*261 Kneeling Nude   (1918)
Nu accroupi
Etching Pl. 104   Essai   6⅛ ×2⅛″
Jean Matisse, Paris

262 Marguerite, eyes closed   (1919)
Marguerite les yeux fermés,
Etching Pl. 108   Essai   3¼ ×5⅝″
Jean Matisse, Paris
Reproduced: L. p.50 (right)

263 Nude Seated in an Armchair   (1922)
Nu assis dans un fauteuil
Lithograph Pl. 30   26/50   15½ ×10″
University of California, Los Angeles,
Norton Simon Collection

264 Seated Nude, Right Hand on Hip   (1922)
Nu assis, main droite à la hanche
Lithograph Pl. 31   41/50   15½ × 9¾″
University of California, Los Angeles,
Norton Simon Collection

265 Young Girl and Vase of Anemones   (1922)
Jeune fille à la table aux anémones
Lithograph Pl. 34   43/50   15¹¹/₁₆ × 11¹/₁₆″
University of California, Los Angeles,
Norton Simon Collection

*266 Reclining Nude on a Chaise Longue   (1922)
Nu au canapé
Lithograph Pl. 35   21/50   19⅜ ×15¾″
University of California, Los Angeles,
Grunwald Graphic Arts Foundation

*267 Female Nude   (1922)
Jeune fille nue
Lithograph Pl. 37   35/50   15 ×9½″
University of California, Los Angeles,
Norton Simon Collection

268 The Organdy Dress   (1922)
La robe en organdi
Lithograph Pl. 38   16/50   16¾ ×10¹³/₁₆″
Mr. and Mrs. Sidney F. Brody, Los Angeles
Reproduced: L. p.100

*269 Odalisque with Magnolias   (1923)
Odalisque aux magnolias
Lithograph Pl. 42   Essai   11¼ ×15¾″
University of California, Los Angeles.
Norton Simon Collection

270 Odalisque in Striped Pantaloons, Reflected in a
Mirror   (1923)
Odalisque à culotte rayée, reflétée dans la glace
Lithograph Pl. 43   7/10   15½ ×11″
University of California, Los Angeles,
Norton Simon Collection
Reproduced: Berg. 1954

271 Odalisque with a Necklace   (1923)
Odalisque au collier
Lithograph Pl. 44   6/10   9 ×12¼″
University of California, Los Angeles.
Norton Simon Collection

272 Reclining Nude, Right Arm Behind Head   (1923)
Odalisque couchée, bras droit derrière la tête
Lithograph Pl. 47   8/10   5½ ×7½″
University of California, Los Angeles,
Norton Simon Collection

273 Reclining Nude, Left Arm Behind Head   (1923)
Odalisque couchée, bras gauche derrière la tête
Lithograph Pl. 48   2/10   5½ ×8″
University of California, Los Angeles,
Norton Simon Collection

274 Young Girl Reading   (1923)
La Liseuse
Lithograph Pl. 49   4/12   19¼ ×15¼″
University of California, Los Angeles,
Norton Simon Collection
Reproduced: Berg 1954

*275 Girl with a Vase of Flowers   (1923)
Jeune fille au vase de fleurs
Lithograph Pl. 51   55/60   10⅞ ×7½″
Mr. and Mrs. Sidney F. Brody, Los Angeles

276 Seated Odalisque, Arms Behind Head (1923-24)
Odalisque assise, bras derrière la tête
Lithograph Pl. 52 7/10 14½×10¾″
University of California, Los Angeles,
Norton Simon Collection

*277 Seated Nude with Arms Raised (1924)
Nu assis aux bras levés
Lithograph Pl. 55 9/10 24¼×18¹³/₁₆″
Mr. and Mrs. Sidney F. Brody, Los Angeles

278 Woman Leaning on her Right Elbow (1924)
Figure appuyée sur le coude, paravent XVIIᵉ siècle
Lithograph Pl. 57 4/10 12×9½″
University of California, Los Angeles,
Norton Simon Collection
Reproduced: Berg 1954

279 Arabesque (1924)
Arabesque
Lithograph Pl. 58 20/50 19×12½″
University of California, Los Angeles,
Norton Simon Collection
Reproduced: L. *p.106*

280 Seated Nude with Raised Arms (1925)
Nu assis aux bras levés
Lithograph Pl. 63 28/50 25×19″
The Art Institute of Chicago,
The Albert Rouiller Memorial Collection
Reproduced: L. *p.109*; B. *p.445*

*281 Odalisque in Striped Pantaloons (1925)
La culotte bayadère
Lithograph Pl. 64 8/10 21¼×17¼″
University of California, Los Angeles,
Norton Simon Collection

282 Interior with Woman Reading (1925)
Intérieur, la lecture
Lithograph Pl. 65 42/50 10⅝×7½″
University of California, Los Angeles,
Grunwald Graphic Arts Foundation
Reproduced: Berg 1954

283 Reclining Odalisque with Basket of Fruit (1925)
Odalisque couchée au panier de fruits
Lithograph Pl. 66 2/10 7½×10½″
University of California, Los Angeles,
Norton Simon Collection

284 Study of Legs (1925)
Etude de jambes
Lithograph Pl. 71 47/50 9¾×19¾″
Jean Matisse, Paris
Reproduced: L. *p.105 (bottom)*; B. *p.445*

*285 Seated Nude, Left Knee Raised (1925)
Nu assis, jambe gauche levée
Lithograph Pl. 75 27/50 19½×16½″
University of California, Los Angeles,
Norton Simon Collection

286 Seated Nude with Arms Behind Head (1925)
Nu assis dans un fauteuil, les deux bras derrière la tête
Lithograph Pl. 77 24/25 12½×9¼″
University of California, Los Angeles,
Norton Simon Collection

287 Girl Reading (Marguerite) (1925)
Marguerite lisant
Lithograph Pl. 78 18/50 6¼×9¾″
University of California, Los Angeles,
Norton Simon Collection
Reproduced: L. *p.99*

*288 Portrait of Cortot (1926)
Drypoint Pl. 106 8/15 5⅜ × 3⁵/₁₆″
University of California, Los Angeles,
Grunwald Graphic Arts Foundation

*289 Alfred Cortot (1927)
Lithograph Pl. 82 15/50 15×11½″
University of California, Los Angeles,
Norton Simon Collection

290 Dancer Reflected in a Mirror (1927)
Danseuse reflétée dans la glace
Lithograph Pl. 87 20/50 15½×10¾″
University of California, Los Angeles,
Norton Simon Collection
Reproduced: Berg 1954

291 Nude with Decorative Background (1927)
Torse à l'aiguière
Lithograph Pl. 88 22/50 14½×10¼″
University of California, Los Angeles,
Norton Simon Collection
Reproduced: Berg 1954

*292 Two Odalisques (1928)
Deux odalisques
Lithograph Pl. 109 49/50 18×30″
University of California, Los Angeles,
Grunwald Graphic Arts Foundation

*293 Reclining Nude with Louis XV Table (1929)
Nu renversé, table Louis XV
Lithograph Pl. 118 27/50 22×18″
University of California, Los Angeles,
Norton Simon Collection

*294 Seated Nude, Left Knee Drawn to Chest (192
Femme nue serrant son genou gauche contre sa poitrine
Drypoint Pl. 116 20/25 5¹³/₁₆×4″
University of California, Los Angeles,
Grunwald Graphic Arts Foundation

295 Woman's Head Resting on Left Arm (1929)
Femme, visage reposant sur le bras gauche, fond à carreaux
Etching Pl. 92 21/25 5½×8¾″
University of California, Los Angeles,
Norton Simon Collection

*296 Seated Woman, Arms on Knees (1929)
Figure assise, bras sur les genoux
Etching Pl. 97 18/25 7⅞×5⅞″
University of California, Los Angeles,
Norton Simon Collection

297   Seated Figure with Necklace   (1929)

Figure assise au collier
Etching Pl. 98   *Essai*   8⁹/₁₆×6″
University of California, Los Angeles,
Grunwald Graphic Arts Foundation

298   Head of a Woman, Full Face   (1929)

Femme, tête de face
Etching Pl. 100 bis   22/25   9¾×6⅞″
University of California, Los Angeles,
Norton Simon Collection

*299   Woman Seated, Hands on Back of Chair   (1929)

Figure assise, mains sur le dos du fauteuil
Etching Pl. 126   20/25   6×4¾″
University of California, Los Angeles,
Norton Simon Collection

300   Profile of a Nude with Head Turned   (1929)

Nu, profil, tête renversée
Etching Pl. 138   23/25   4¼×5¾″
University of California, Los Angeles,
Norton Simon Collection

301   Woman, Profile, Beside an Aquarium   (1929)

Femme en profil, près d'un aquarium
Etching Pl. 140   Etat   3⅜×6″
Jean Matisse, Paris

302   Nude, Lying on Her Side   (1929)

Nu couché sur le côté
Etching Pl. 141   22/25   3¾×5⅝″
University of California, Los Angeles,
Norton Simon Collection

*303   Woman, Full Face, Beside an Aquarium   (1929)

Femme de face, près d'un aquarium
Etching Pl. 142   25/25   3⅜×5″
Jean Matisse, Paris

304   Seated Woman with Clasped Hands, Patterned
Background   (1929)

Femme assise, mains croisées, fond à carreaux
Etching Pl. 145   25/25   4⅜×5⅞″
Mr. and Mrs. Sidney F. Brody, Los Angeles

305   Woman Leaning on Her Right Elbow   (1929)

Femme accoudée sur le bras droit
Etching Pl. 146 bis   22/25   6⅛×8½″
University of California, Los Angeles,
Norton Simon Collection

*306   Head of a Woman with Bowl of Fish   (1929)

Tête penchée, bocal de poissons
Etching Pl. 150   22/25   5¾×7½″
University of California, Los Angeles,
Norton Simon Collection

307   Woman, Full Face, Bow on Side of Neck   (1929)

Figure de face, nœud de ruban à côté de cou
Etching Pl. 157   18/25   6⅞×4½″
University of California, Los Angeles,
Norton Simon Collection

*308   Seated Girl with Bowl of Fish   (1929)

Nu assis, bocal de poissons
Etching Pl. 179   23/25   5⅞×8¾″
Mr. and Mrs. Sidney F. Brody, Los Angeles

309   Seated Nude, Three-Quarter View   (1929)

Nu assis de trois quarts
Etching Pl. 181   22/25   9¾×3⅞″
University of California, Los Angeles,
Norton Simon Collection

310   Seated Nude, Hand on Shoulder   (1929)

Nu accroupi, main sur l'épaule
Etching Pl. 185   20/25   9¾×6½″
University of California, Los Angeles,
Norton Simon Collection

311   Young Girl with Cage of Parakeets   (1929)

Jeune fille et cage de perruches
Etching Pl. 186   13/25   9¼×6½″
University of California, Los Angeles,
Norton Simon Collection

312   Seated Nude in Tulle Jacket   (1929)

Nu assis, chemise tulle
Lithograph Pl. 69   45/50   14¼×10½″
The Fred Grunwald Collection, Los Angeles

*313   Persian Girl   (1929)

La Persane
Lithograph Pl. 100   16/50   17×11″
University of California, Los Angeles,
Norton Simon Collection

314   Persian Girl   (1930)

La Persane
Lithograph Pl. 125   44/75   17¼×12¼″
University of California, Los Angeles,
Norton Simon Collection
Reproduced: L. *p.118*

315   Head of a Woman, Full Face   (1930)

Figure, femme de face
Lithograph Pl. 151   22/25   4⅞×⅞″
University of California, Los Angeles,
Norton Simon Collection

316   Head of a Woman, Patterned Background   (1931)

Tête de femme, fond à carreaux
Etching Pl. 162   23/25   4¾×3⅝″
University of California, Los Angeles,
Norton Simon Collection

317   Seated Nude, Venetian Lamp and Goldfish Bowl
(1931)

Nu assis, lampe vénitienne et poissons rouges
Etching Pl. 165   17/25   7¾×5⅞″
University of California, Los Angeles,
Norton Simon Collection

*318   Self Portrait   (1936)

Auto-portrait
Lithograph, No plate number   4/10   13×10″
The Art Institute of Chicago

*319 Siesta (1937)
La sieste
Linoleum cut Pl. 247   24/25   10¼ × 12″
University of California, Los Angeles,
Norton Simon Collection

*320 The Beautiful Tahitian (1937)
La belle Tahitienne
Linoleum cut Pl. 255   22/25   11 × 7¾″
University of California, Los Angeles,
Norton Simon Collection

321 Head of a Woman (1938)
Tête de femme
Linoleum cut Pl. 243   22/25   7½ × 6¾″
University of California, Los Angeles,
Norton Simon Collection

322 Woman, Thumb on Mouth (1938)
Femme, pouce sur la bouche
Linoleum cut Pl. 256   24/25   11¼ × 7¾″
University of California, Los Angeles,
Norton Simon Collection

323 Pot of Begonias (1938)
Pot à bégonias
Linoleum cut Pl. 257   16/25   7⅞ × 9″
Mr. and Mrs. Sidney F. Brody, Los Angeles
Reproduced: Berg 1952 *No. 21*

324 Heads (1939)
Têtes
Etching Pl. 258   12/20   2 × 9¾″
University of California, Los Angeles,
Norton Simon Collection

*325 Head (Full Face) (1948)
Tête de face
Aquatint Pl. 342   5/25   12⅜ × 9⅞″
The Museum of Modern Art, New York,
Curt Valentin Bequest

*326 Head (Profile) (1948)
Aquatint Pl. 359   16/25   16¹⁵/₁₆ × 13¾″
The Museum of Modern Art, New York,
Curt Valentin Bequest

327 Face of a Woman (1949)
Visage d'une femme
Etching Pl. 301   15/25   9⅞ × 7⅝″
University of California, Los Angeles,
Grunwald Graphic Arts Foundation

328 Carmen, Three-quarter Face (1949)
Carmen, visage de trois quarts
Etching Pl. 310   15/25   5¹¹/₁₆ × 4⁵/₁₆″
University of California, Los Angeles,
Grunwald Graphic Arts Foundation
Reproduced: Berg 1952   *No. 12*

329 Face of a Woman (1949)
Visage
Lithograph Pl. 362   78/200   15¹¹/₁₆ × 12¹¹/₁₆″
The Fred Grunwald Collection, Los Angeles

330 Stéphane Mallarmé. *Poésies de Stéphane Mallarmé*
Lausanne: Albert Skira et Cie.   1932
Printer: Roger Lacourière, etchings
         Léon Picon, text
Edition: 1 leaf, 153 pp, 4 leaves including 29 etchi
printed in black. Page size 13 × 10″
Limited, signed and numbered 6   (95)
The Brooklyn Museum

331 James Joyce. *Ulysses*
New York: The Limited Editions Club   1935
Printer: The Limited Editions Club
Designer: George Macy
Edition: xv, (1) pp, 1 leaf, 368 pp including
6 soft-ground etchings printed in black, each w
2-5 reproduction of preliminary drawings
Page size 11¾ × 9″
Limited, signed and numbered 992   (1500)
Library of the University of California, Los Ang

332 Henri Matisse. *Jazz*
(Paris) Teriade   (1947)
Printer: Edmond Vairel, stencils
         Draeger Frères, text
Edition: 146 pp, 4 leaves including 20 stencils v
15 double-page, printed in color after collages
and gouaches découpées. Page size 16½ × 12¾″
Limited, signed and numbered 104   (250)
University of California, Los Angeles,
Norton Simon Collection

333 Pierre de Ronsard. *Florilège des amours de Ronsard*
(Paris) Albert Skira et Cie.   (1948)
Printer: Mourlot Frères, lithography
         Georges Girard, text
Designer: Henri Matisse with the collaboration
Marc Barraud
Edition: 185 (1) pp, 2 leaves including
126 lithographs; 125 printed in sanguine, 1 in b
Cover: lithograph in sanguine
Page size 15 × 11″
Limited, signed and numbered 60   (320)
This copy inscribed (leaf opposite half-title page)
"pour Peter Matisse | H. Matisse | Nice fév. 49″
an original color crayon drawing
(half-title page), by the artist.
University of California, Los Angeles,
Norton Simon Collection

334 Charles d'Orléans. *Poèmes de Charles d'Orléans*
(Paris) Teriade   (1950)
Printer: Mourlot Frères, lithography
Edition: 100 pp, 2 leaves including 54 lithogr
printed in color
Text lithographed in the hand writing of the ar
Page size 16 × 10⅜″
Limited, signed and numbered 1020   (1200)
University of California, Los Angeles,
Norton Simon Collection

GOUACHES DÉCOUPÉES

*335   Still Life   (1941)
Nature morte
23⅝"×32"
Pierre Matisse

*336   Front Design for Priest's Black Vestment,
Vence Chapel
(for execution in appliquéd cloth)   (1949-50)
Chasuble noire
50×78"
Musée Matisse, Cimiez-Nice
Reproduced: M.W. p. 12

337   Back Design for Priest's Black Vestment,
Vence Chapel
(for execution in appliquéd cloth)   (1949-50)
Chasuble noire
50×78"
Musée Matisse, Cimiez-Nice

338   Snow Flowers   1951
Fleurs de neige
68⅛×31⅞"   Signed and dated lower right
Private Collection, Paris
Reproduced: V. p. 21; M.W. p. 21

339   Vegetables   1951 (signed in 1952)
Végétaux
68⅞×32¼"   Signed and dated lower right
Jean Matisse, Paris
Reproduced: V. p. 20; M.W. p. 20

340   Standing Blue Nude   (1952)
Nu bleu
44½×29"
Pierre Matisse
Reproduced: V. p. 20; M.W. p. 20

341   Seated Blue Nude II   1952
Nu bleu II
45¾×35"   Signed and dated lower right
Pierre Matisse
Reproduced: V. p. 106; M.W. p. 22 (left)

*342   Seated Blue Nude III   1952
Nu bleu III
45¾×32"   Signed and dated lower center
Jean Matisse, Paris
Reproduced: V. p. 107; M.W. p. 22 (right)

*343   Seated Blue Nude IV   1952
Nu bleu IV
40½×30¼"   Signed and dated lower center
Jean Matisse, Paris
Reproduced: V. p. 109; M. W. p. 23

344   Nude with Oranges   (1953)
Nu aux oranges
Gouache découpée and India ink   60×42"
Signed lower right
Pierre Matisse
Reproduced: Verve *frontispiece*; M.W. p. 34

*345   The Sheaf (designed for wall ceramic)   1953
La gerbe
115¾"×137¾"   Signed and dated lower right
UCLA Art Galleries, Los Angeles
Reproduced: V. pp. 148-149

*All Gouaches Découpées are gouaches on cut-and-pasted-paper,
unless otherwise indicated.*

*Whenever possible, reproduction references from the
following books are indicated below, for those gouaches
not herein reproduced:*

M.W.   Monroe Wheeler, *The Last Works of Matisse—
Large Cut Gouaches* (New York; The Museum of
Modern Art, 1961)

V.   Verve, *The Last Works of Matisse*
(New York: Harcourt, Brace and Co., 1958)
All reproductions in *Verve* are in color.

Selection of objects used as models in the works
of Henri Matisse, Musée Matisse, Cimiez-Nice

Lenders to Henri Matisse Retrospective Exhibition 1966

Albright-Knox Art Gallery, Buffalo
The Art Institute of Chicago
Mr. and Mrs. Lee A. Ault, New York
Dr. and Mrs. Harry Bakwin, New York
The Baltimore Museum of Art
Heinz Berggruen, Paris
Berner Kunstmuseum, Bern
Galerie Beyeler, Basel
Mrs. Robert Woods Bliss, Washington, D.C.
Mr. and Mrs Leigh B. Block, Chicago
Museum of Fine Arts, Boston
Mr. and Mrs. Sidney F. Brody, Los Angeles
The Brooklyn Museum
City Art Museum of St. Louis
Mr. and Mrs. Ralph F. Colin, New York
Mr. and Mrs. Alfred Cowles, Lake Forest, Illinois
Mr. and Mrs. Nathan Cummings, Chicago
Mr. and Mrs. Richard S. Davis, London
The Detroit Institute of Arts
Mrs. Marcel Duchamp, New York
Monsieur and Madame Georges Duthuit, Paris
Dr. and Mrs. David I. Elterman, Sherman Oaks, Calif.
Fogg Art Museum, Harvard University, Cambridge
Mr. and Mrs. William Goetz, Los Angeles
The Gothenberg Art Gallery, Gothenberg, Sweden
Grenoble Musée de Peinture et de Sculpture
The Fred Grunwald Collection
Mr. and Mrs. Walter A. Haas, San Francisco
Professor Hans R. Hahnloser, Bern
The Alex Hillman Corporation, New York
The Joseph H. Hirshhorn Collection, New York
Mrs. Albert D. Lasker, New York
Monsieur Pierre Lévy, Troyes, France
Wright Saltus Ludington, Santa Barbara, California
Monsieur Jean Matisse, Paris
Mr. and Mrs. Pierre Matisse, New York
P. N. Matisse Gallery, Beverly Hills
The Metropolitan Museum of Art, New York

The Minneapolis Institute of Arts
Musée d'Art Moderne de la Ville de Paris
Musée Matisse, Cimiez-Nice
Musée National d'Art Moderne, Paris
The Museum of Modern Art, New York
Dr. and Mrs. Franklin D. Murphy, Los Angeles
Mrs. Charles S. Payson, Manhasset, Long Island
Frank Perls, Beverly Hills
Philadelphia Museum of Art
Mr. and Mrs. Gifford Phillips, Santa Monica, California
The Phillips Collection, Washington, D.C.
Monsieur and Madame Pablo Picasso, Mougins, France
Mr. and Mrs. James E. Pollak, Los Angeles
Mr. and Mrs. Otto Preminger, New York
Mr. and Mrs. Joseph Pulitzer, Jr., St. Louis
Mr. and Mrs. John Rewald, New York
Paul Rosenberg and Company, New York
Siegfried Rosengart, Lucerne
Sam Salz, New York
The San Francisco Museum of Art
The Santa Barbara Museum of Art
Mr. and Mrs. Taft Schreiber, Beverly Hills
Mr. and Mrs. Norton Simon, Los Angeles
Charles E. Slatkin Galleries, New York
Mrs. Vicci Sperry, Los Angeles
Mrs. Bertram Smith, New York
Mr. and Mrs. Ray Stark, Los Angeles
The Trustees of The Tate Gallery, London
Mrs. Hildegard Ault Tjeder
University of California, Los Angeles, Art Galleries
University of California, Los Angeles, Library
University of California, Los Angeles,
  Grunwald Graphic Arts Foundation
University of California, Los Angeles,
  Norton Simon Collection
Mrs. John Wintersteen, President,
  Philadelphia Museum of Art

Schedule for Henri Matisse Retrospective Exhibition 1966

UCLA Art Galleries, January 5 – February 27
The Art Institute of Chicago, March 11 – April
Museum of Fine Arts, Boston, May 11 – June 26

Printed in Swit

Lay-out by Pierre Faucheux, Paris

Printed December 15th 1965 on the Press
of the Imprimeries Réunies S.A. Lausanne Switzerland
Engraving by Bussière, Arts Graphiques